MOTHER *of* PURL

MOTHER *of* PURL

FRIENDS, FUN, AND FABULOUS DESIGNS AT HOLLYWOOD'S KNITTING CIRCLE

EDITH EIG

with *Caroline Greeven*

PHOTOS BY Warren Eig

Collins

An Imprint of HarperCollinsPublishers

HarperCollins books may be purchased for educational, business, or sales promotional use. For information please write: Special Markets Department, HarperCollins Publishers, 10 East 53rd Street, New York, NY 10022.

FIRST EDITION

Photos and graphics by Warren L. Eig
Designed by Vertigo Design

Eig, Edith.
    Mother of purl : friends, fun and fabulous designs at Hollywood's knitting circle /Edith Eig with Caroline Greeven.
        p. cm.
    Includes index.
    ISBN-10: 0-06-081827-1
    ISBN-13: 978-0-06-081827-2
    1. Knitting–Patterns. I. Greeven, Caroline. II. Title
    TT820.E52 2005
    746.43'2041–dc22   2005046248

05 06 07 08 09 ❖/RRD 10 9 8 7 6 5 4 3 2 1

contents

Acknowledgments   viii

introduction
BRINGING CHIC WITHIN YOUR REACH   x

chapter one
THE BASICS   1

chapter two
THE NEXT STEP   21

chapter three
EXPLORING YARNS   37

chapter four
KNITTING TECHNIQUES   47

chapter five
PERFECT FINISHING   59

chapter six
EMOTIONAL KNITTING   69

chapter seven
SIP & KNIT: PULL UP A CHAIR   77

chapter eight
KNITTING FOR OTHERS   81

chapter nine
THE FUTURE OF KNITTING   85

chapter ten
PATTERNS   91

Glossary of Terms   210
Abbreviations   214
Knitting Needle Table   215
Resource List   216
Index   218

"Because Edith is such a nice and patient teacher, I learned to knit."

—Sofia Coppola

"I always wanted to knit, but never thought I could until I met Edith. Her patience and kindness has opened a whole new world for me."

—Daryl Hannah

"Knitting is a nice way to relax and be productive at the same time."

—Julianne Moore

"I am so pleased that knitting has made a comeback. It is an art, and it is a pleasure, and thank heaven for Edith and La Knitterie Parisienne—it's a knitter's paradise."

—Shelley Morrison

"I just love to knit and love to knit with Edith because she knows everything in the world about knitting. I remember the first time I went to Edith's La Knitterie Parisienne . . . I went four days in a row. And, if I make a mistake, I can't wait to call Edith or go to the store so she can help me. Knitting is so much fun, and I can't wait to learn to knit ponchos and sweaters for my stuffed dogs because I don't have a real one. My next project is going to be a yellow scarf for my grandmother."

—Dakota Fanning

"Edith is the Deepak Chopra of knitting. She'll take you from pot holder to cable-knit sweaters in no time."

—Caroline Rhea

"Knitting is a family tradition."

—Bridget Fonda

"I learned to knit as a little girl but gave it up over the years. Edith helped me rediscover the love and passion I had for this creative hobby and I haven't stopped knitting since."

—Hilary Shephard

"I can't imagine life without knitting, and it has always amazed me that more people don't do it. Edith Eig's La Knitterie Parisienne is the most welcoming knit shop I have ever been in."

—Annette O'Toole

"Edith is incredibly helpful and giving of her knitting skills and experience. I wouldn't know much about knitting or crocheting without her. She's incredibly encouraging and one of my favorite people on earth."

—Justine Bateman

"Edith Eig is the owner of La Knitterie Parisienne in Studio City, the hottest, trendiest place in town for the young set to gather and knit. Knitting with Edith is the place to be."

—KNBC-TV

"Edith is a master knitter; she is known as the best in the world."

—KCBS-TV

"Hollywood's knitting guru is Edith Eig."

—*People* magazine

"La Knitterie Parisienne is Southern California's largest and most fashionable knitting yarn boutique."

—*Los Angeles* magazine

"Mme Eig has emerged as a guru to whom studios and actors turn for practical help and spiritual solace."

—*The London Times*

"Edith Eig, knitting guru, takes life one stitch at a time."

—*Los Angeles Times*

"La Knitterie Parisienne is run by knitting-instructor-to-the-stars Edith Eig."

—*Los Angeles Daily News*

"In the hustle-bustle, ultra-chic world that is Hollywood, one of the hottest spots is La Knitterie Parisienne, where the stars go to unwind, enter a simpler world, and find joy in a pastime that many of their grandmothers practiced."

—*Costco Connection* magazine

acknowledgments

This book is dedicated to my husband, Merrill, to my daughters, Audrey and Natalie, and to my son, Warren. Without their help, inspiration, and guidance, this book would not have been possible. In my thirty years of business, I have had the pleasure of meeting and getting to know thousands upon thousands of knitters from all over the world. To them and all my customers—many of whom have become good friends— I thank you.

In particular, I must thank my "Knitting Friends" for their patience, input, and willing ears as I created these wonderful and original designs for my book. The list of people to thank is endless, and I apologize if I have forgotten anyone.

But to those who have contributed to this book, I am very grateful: Yoli Poropat, for your help in typing my patterns. Art Anthony, for your talented makeup artistry in making me look like a movie star. Haley Alexander, for creating my signature red nails. Roslyn Rothenberg, my dear friend, who travels across the country just to buy yarn—I love you. Nora Welten, your friendship and support have been invaluable. Thank you, Amy Whetsel, my wonderful assistant, for always being there when you could.

A special thank you to all my good friends and clients who took the time to model my creations and make them look even more beautiful: Semara Lapchinski, Brenda and Ivan Lapchinski, Carolyn Hennesy, Anel Gorham, Christopher Gorham, Mary Chris Wall, Nancy Schnoll, Carnie Wilson, Miriam Peguero, J. Robin Miller, Shellie Kleiman, Doris Stoller, and Antoinette Spolar-Levine. Thank you also to Daryl Hannah, Shelley Morrison, Hilary Shepard, Kellie Martin, Hedy Burress, Eliza Thorne, Jodi Gechtman, and Tal Meirson. A special thanks to Laura Lamers for your constant help and your innovativeness that entices the customers into creativity.

Thank you, Beverly Dalton, for your lovely floral arrangements, for your "spirits," and for always keeping me in the know. To Bonnie Auerbach, a big thank you for hosting our holiday party, and Steve Sfetku for helping to set up our photo shoot.

Thank you to all the yarn manufacturers and distributors who have helped to fill my store with their beautiful yarns. To my good friends, Barry and Myrna Klein from Trendsetters, thank you for your yarn contribution, friendship, and support. To Brad and Jeannine Duncan of Fiesta Yarns for the lovely gift of cashmere, Lusso and Tenero. Thank you to the team at Knitting Fever and Euro Yarn. A special thank you to Mr. Okada and Jan Carr of Clover Needles for listening to me and always giving me support; and to Margorie Winters and Warren Warlock of Berroco, Inc., for creating the "Edith Coat."

And last, but never least, a big kiss to my fine feathered friends, Oscar and George, and my canine model, Leo.

introduction

BRINGING CHIC WITHIN YOUR REACH

Bringing sophisticated knitting to people who never imagined they could be creative, never thought they could make something beautiful, that is my mission. Nothing makes me happier than helping a knitter toward success.

I feel I have been writing this book for over thirty years. After all, knitting has been a part of my life since I was a young girl in France, when knitting was part of the curriculum and I was forced to sit indoors "_à l'école_" and knit, while the boys got to go outside and play. This always seemed terribly unfair to me—_I_ wanted to go out and play; what did I care about knitting?—and as soon as I graduated I threw away my needles. When I turned eighteen, I moved to America, got married, and became a career woman, working in finance at a brokerage firm on Wall Street. Knitting—or any kind of craft, for that matter—could not have been further from my mind; who had time?

So, in a way, I guess my knitting life is typical of many women; a craft that we may not think of for years, and then suddenly it starts to make sense—one day we find that there is something missing in our lives, and knitting helps fill the void. For me, I began to feel the _need_ to knit when I left the professional world to become a mother; where once my busy days had been filled with conversation and intellectually demanding work, I now found myself alone for much of the day, with just my young children for company, or the occasional coffee klatch, which, to be honest, bored me out of my mind. One day I bought a pair of needles, some yarn, and sat down and knitted a baby blanket. I've been knitting ever since.

Soon I was showing my friends how to knit their own baby blankets, and as we sipped coffee, I found I enjoyed teaching them, and started to enjoy having a creative circle of my contemporaries. We were friends when we began knitting, and just as our stitches became intertwined, so did the bonds of our friendship over needles and yarn. I found I had a knack for teaching and a love for needlecrafts; a local school invited me to teach there, and when I started ordering supplies for my students, I realized the next step was my own store. The Canvas Pad, which I opened in the basement of my home in Parsippany, New Jersey, was a complete resource for all needlecrafts—both knitting and needlepoint. My knitting circle picked up and relocated to my new business, and gradually more people joined us.

Every night my husband, Merrill, would come home from work to find dozens of women in our house, and more often than not, they would end up staying for dinner as well. The store grew gradually, but it was always a success, and I soon moved from our basement to a store that was so little I had to stand outside the entrance way if I had more than one customer. Over time, the Canvas Pad moved to bigger and bigger locations, finally establishing a more than twenty-year residency in a 218-year-old historic Victorian house. The Canvas Pad, which began as a hobby, had evolved into a pretty impressive business. Not bad for something I started on a whim!

Our children grew up and moved to Los Angeles. Eventually, Merrill and I moved too, carefully packing up every last skein of yarn and relocating our business. We found a home in the San Fernando Valley, and soon after that a perfect location in Studio City. La Knitterie

Parisienne was born, and the new name for the business was created to reflect my Parisienne sensibilities while clearly establishing the nature of the shop.

I had a brand-new opportunity to reestablish my knitting yarn business, and I wanted to offer my clients the highest-quality yarns available on the market. Throughout my career, I had honed my abilities as a skilled designer with a sophisticated flair for style and color. A mother of three, I also found that I had acquired the art of patience and had a natural ability to teach—both novice and expert knitters alike. This was a time before the knitting revival, and my new clientele was gravitating to the warmth and charm of my shop. It was comforting and rewarding; after all, Merrill and I had taken a huge risk in moving our successful business cross-country, and now new customers were finding a new home at La Knitterie Parisienne surrounded by one of the largest inventories ever found in a single shop: 13,000 yarns and, without exception, one of the best in the market.

Coincidentally, La Knitterie Parisienne was located in the heart of the movie studio district: Universal Studios, Warner Brothers, Walt Disney Studios, Raleigh Studios, and Paramount Pictures, to name a few, were just a stone's throw away. As a result, I found much of my clientele comprised the stars and tastemakers of Hollywood, and they, like the rest of my customers, demanded the best.

This was an eye-opening experience for me, having operated a successful business in sub-

GOOD KARMA

One of my clients, an actress and model, regularly stops at my shop on her way to auditions because she claims my store provides her with "good karma." In the many years that she has performed this ritual, she always got the part.

urban New Jersey, where most of my clients were professionals and stay-at-home moms. The mix had now broadened to include a circle of celebrities, movie producers and directors, screenwriters, stylists and makeup artists: today's trendsetters who appear in the pages of high fashion and entertainment magazines and are partly responsible for helping to launch what is considered popular.

Because I was in the forefront of the knitting renaissance, I have had an unprecedented involvement in the evolution of my craft. I have worked closely with yarn manufacturers and needle companies to help them develop new lines, and have given them a perspective on what clients really want and need, as well as what doesn't work. In a way, it was as if yarn was flowing through my veins and I was able to connect with my customers, offering them resources they couldn't find elsewhere. I became adept at designing patterns for my clients when they couldn't find interesting ones in existing books and magazines. I was unmotivated by the ordinary; I wanted the extraordinary, and so did my clients. Since its inception, La Knitterie Parisienne has been known for its incredible selection of inventory, its excellent customer service, and now for my original one-of-a-kind designs.

As word spread about my shop, people were traveling from all distances to share in the experience. From their first foot in the door, they were hooked, sitting alongside fellow knitters—whom they'd soon call friends—at the large circular wooden table in the center of the store. The press wasn't immune to our popularity, and they too became involved by reporting on this newfound knitting phenomenon. I had been touted by syndicated columnist Liz Smith as the pied piper of knitting, and word was traveling fast among the media that had crowned me the "guru of knitting" and my shop as the place to knit. My reputation as a leader within the knitting yarn industry catapulted La Knitterie Parisienne into the headlines, with media coverage in local, national, and international print and broadcast outlets.

La Knitterie Parisienne became the *it* place to sit and knit, ultimately helping to popularize the idea of the knitting circle—a place to find fun, friends, fashion, and fiber all in one spot.

Now, for the first time, I am gathering everything I have learned over the years into one complete resource: *Mother of Purl: Friends, Fun, and Fabulous Designs at Hollywood's Knitting Circle.* More than just a pattern book, *Mother of Purl* is a sophisticated knitting book, showcasing my techniques and tips that will encourage you to explore your own creativity and incite a passion to knit some really incredible designs—designs that I have created especially for this book. From my couture-worthy ponchos, suits, skirts, dresses, shrugs, and jackets to a pink bikini, tank tops, blankets, and the ultimate diaper bag—which I'm introducing for the very first time—I hope *Mother of Purl* will inspire you to begin knitting or motivate you to further improve your knitting skills, whether you're a novice or a seasoned knitter.

You won't find ten methods of casting on or eight options for creating a buttonhole in *Mother of Purl.* Instead, I am offering you an inspirational resource book of the tried-and-true methods that I teach my clients every day in my store. I have created elegant designs with simple, easy-to-follow instructions that I am delighted to be able to share with you.

I truly believe that knitting can enrich one's life, from meeting new friends, stimulating an artistic outlet, strengthening self-expression, and creating beautiful hand-knitted items.

The art of knitting transcends the basic knit one, purl one concept and inspires a continuing curiosity and desire to learn. I am an advocate for learning; it makes us better people. It is my hope that *Mother of Purl* will inspire you to keep learning and will guide you through the interesting tricks of the trade I offer my customers when we sit and knit—and even rip—until we are satisfied with what we have created.

I designed this book to appeal to knitters of every level, and my ultimate goal is to make you feel like you're a knitter and a client sitting at my table among friends at La Knitterie Parisienne. *Mother of Purl* will both teach the basic elements of knitting and offer more advanced knitters the tried-and-true tips and techniques that I have cultivated over the years.

As you read through *Mother of Purl,* you'll notice that this book has been set up to give you a sense of La Knitterie Parisienne's style of knitting. My signature designs are found in the second half of the book with step-by-step instructions and photographs.

chapter one

THE BASICS

My philosophy is to help knitters find the joy in

creating something of substance and style—

something that is all your own. It's amazing how

universal knitting can be. I have clients from all

over the world, and even when there are language

barriers, we can communicate through stitches.

La Knitterie Parisienne normally closes at 6:00 p.m., but on most nights the last knitter doesn't leave until hours after that. So I often find myself at the store until eight o'clock at night encouraging a client to learn the purl stitch, or helping her pick the perfect yarn for a project.

On a typical day, I'll teach as many as twenty people or more how to cast on and knit. Their levels of learning vary, as does their confidence. Some students grasp the concept of knitting immediately and can virtually finish a chunky scarf in one sitting, while others may struggle to understand the basic knit stitch and may sit for hours knitting and ripping the same row.

Regardless of these challenges, anyone can learn to knit, and knit well, as long as they have patience. I remind my customers that they must fully understand the basics of knitting and know how to knit and purl before moving on. Like the expression "you must learn to walk before you can run" the same is true for knitting. Equally important, knitters must learn to take one step or, more accurately, one stitch at a time.

Beginners may anticipate the difficulty of purling or creating a sweater, even before they learn the knit stitch. I tell them, why worry about something that you haven't reached yet? Just learn one step at a time, and stick to this philosophy even as you become more experienced—read just a little ahead in the pattern; don't worry about your armholes when you are working on your ribbing.

FIND YOUR LOCAL KNITTING SHOP

When I opened La Knitterie Parisienne in 1996, my goal was to create an atmosphere of warmth, where customers could feel a sense of community, find a wide selection of yarns, and become inspired through example. We strived to create a home away from home, offering caring and personal attention. Unlike walking into a store and simply selecting the blue shirt off the rack, a knitting store is unique in that customers will spend hours upon hours and sometimes consecutive days working on a project, so it's important to feel comfortable with a knowledgeable instructor. La Knitterie Parisienne provides this and more, and it's a place where everyone knows your name!

Knitting makes you able to focus and relax at the same time, and when you have a lot going on in your life, knitting helps to keep things calm and in perspective. When everything else seems to be hectic, it's nice to know that something as simple as knitting can offer instant gratification. Even last night when I was out with good friends, enjoying their company, I couldn't help but think about my latest knitting project. The other guilty pleasure about knitting is that I sit and mindlessly watch TV without feeling as if I'm completely wasting my time. And the thing I absolutely love the most about knitting is knitting with Edith. My whole word changed the day I walked into La Knitterie Parisienne and met Edith to learn how to make a baby blanket. I started my project with the seed stitch—and made quite a few mistakes along the way. Edith—the perfectionist that she is—insisted I

rip. In fact, I ripped and restarted my baby blanket ten times. And you know what? I am so glad she made me do it.

KNITTING ESSENTIALS: THE LEARN TO KNIT KIT

Before we start to knit, I must warn you that like most of us, you may become an addict. But be assured, knitting is an addiction that is safe, nonfattening, and legal. It will also bring you a tremendous amount of pleasure. Side effects have been known to prevent smoking and overeating while increasing your social circle and making numerous new friends.

Like any new activity, knitting requires obtaining the basic necessities before beginning: the proper size needles to ensure the correct gauge, a tape measure, scissors, and, of course, the most impor-

[EDITH KNIT TIP]

Choose Your Yarn Shop Wisely

Investigate your local knitting stores thoroughly–find a place with a nice selection of yarn and accessories and a skilled shop owner or teacher who can answer your questions. In the last year, thousands of knitting stores have opened, but too few of them have the one nonnegotiable item needed for success: a knitting expert. No matter how quaint your local knit shop may be, it will be counterproductive if the owner doesn't know the basics of knitting and is unable to answer questions themselves or guide you through the knitting process to solve your problems.

Having Enough Yarn

When you select the yarn for your project, always make sure that the shop has more in stock than the one ball you select to make your gauge.

Not All 50-Gram Balls Are the Same

The same weight yields different lengths depending on the yarn you choose: 50 grams of acrylic equals 191 yards; 50 grams of wool equals 125 to 130 yards; and 50 grams of cotton equals 115 yards. Always calculate the amount of yarn needed in yards, not ounces or grams.

tant item: a yarn you love. At La Knitterie Parisienne, I only sell the very best quality yarns, needles, books, and patterns. I stock needles that cost as much as $30 a pair, and the finest cashmere yarn costing up to $80 a skein—but I won't sell these items to a beginner. Instead, I recommend first-time knitters start with simple, quality items: a chunky smooth yarn (you'll see your results more quickly) and appropriately sized plastic or bamboo needles. A total initial expenditure should be between $30 and $50.

Yarn. Your first yarn purchase is critical—buy the wrong yarn and you may very well cast knitting aside in frustration and never learn. Buy the right yarn—one that feels soft to the touch and knits up easily—and you will be hooked for life. You'll be amazed at how quickly you'll find yourself bitten by the knitting bug and addicted to the thrill of finding gorgeous new yarns. Once you begin to invest your time in knitting, you'll appreciate the importance of knitting with quality yarns and come to see a $40 skein of yarn as an investment.

Following are basic guidelines to buying yarn for a first project. I will elaborate more on other yarns in the coming chapters, but for now, this is what you will need to know to begin.

- I usually recommend a chunky yarn and one that is soft to the touch and light in color. The key for a first project is to be able to see and recognize each stitch, and at the same time to enjoy seeing your project progress. A light color yarn will also aid in recognizing mistakes.

- Avoid knitting with a fuzzy or hairy yarn, because it will make it hard to see the stitches on your needle. If you make a mistake while knitting with this type of yarn, it is virtually impossible to see the mistake and even more difficult to rip the stitches because the yarn will become completely entangled.

- When offering wool as a choice of yarn, you'd be amazed at how many people say they are allergic to wool, claiming it irritates their skin, when actually

U.S. vs. Metric Needles

When reading your yarn label, make sure the size of the needles stipulated is in U.S. measurements, not metrics; otherwise, you will need to convert it to U.S. sizing. For example, a size 6 metric is actually a size 10 U.S.

A Case for the Needle Case

It's not only functional to keep your knitting needles in the proper needle holder, but it's also extremely practical. If you store and carry your needles in a plastic bag, you may not realize until it's too late, or after the needle has pierced the bag, slipped though, and disappeared. When you go to knit, you find the needle is missing. A needle case protects the needles from breaking, bending, and disappearing.

Pain Relief

If you suffer from arthritis and sometimes find knitting painful, try knitting with Clover bamboo needles. They are lighter in the hand.

they are remembering the coarse scratchy wools they may have worn as a child. Wools have come a long way. Today, most wools are softer and come from a variety of sheep, including the most popular type, merino wool.

- Remember, all wools are not created equal. If it doesn't say 100% Virgin Wool on your label, then it could be made from recycled wool from garments and is of a much lower quality. Virgin wool indicates that it has gone from the sheep to the skein to you, and is much softer since it contains more lanolin and longer fibers, which is a desirable feature. Remember: with wool you get what you pay for.

- If you are looking to felt your knitting, avoid superwash wool. This kind of yarn has been treated and won't shrink.

Needles. Like yarn, there are a variety of knitting needles ranging widely in price and quality. Needles may be made of bamboo, wood, plastic, and metals of all sorts. The Rolls-Royce of needles, however, are the rosewood needles, which are both beautiful and pricey. At La Knitterie Parisienne, I suggest that knitters select needles based on their level of experience. It is not necessary for beginners to use the most expensive needles. Instead, buy a pair of plastic or bamboo needles in the size indicated on the ball of yarn. Often, when knitting a  scarf, I recommend going up one needle size to ensure the scarf is light and airy, and using plastic needles when knitting with artificial fibers, as they don't slide well on bamboo. As you become more experienced, you'll want to invest in needles in a variety of sizes and styles—including the coveted rosewood needles, which also come in incremental sizes. Typically, needles used in the United States only come in single sizes: 0, 1, 2, etc., except for the incremental size of 10.5. For the skilled knitter who wants to be very precise about their knitting gauge, a perfect gauge can be maintained by using rosewood needles, which come in quarter increments such as 8.25 and 8.75. Such sizing is common in Europe.

There are a few other basic items a knitter will need and important to have.

The "Other" Basics.

Besides needles and yarn, other basics include a tape measure, a yarn needle for finishing your garment, scissors, point protectors to prevent the stitches from sliding off the needle, stitch holders, and stitch markers. In addition, I highly recommend purchasing a knitting needle gauge and a stitch counter to keep track of your rows. These come in a variety of styles, and I prefer the

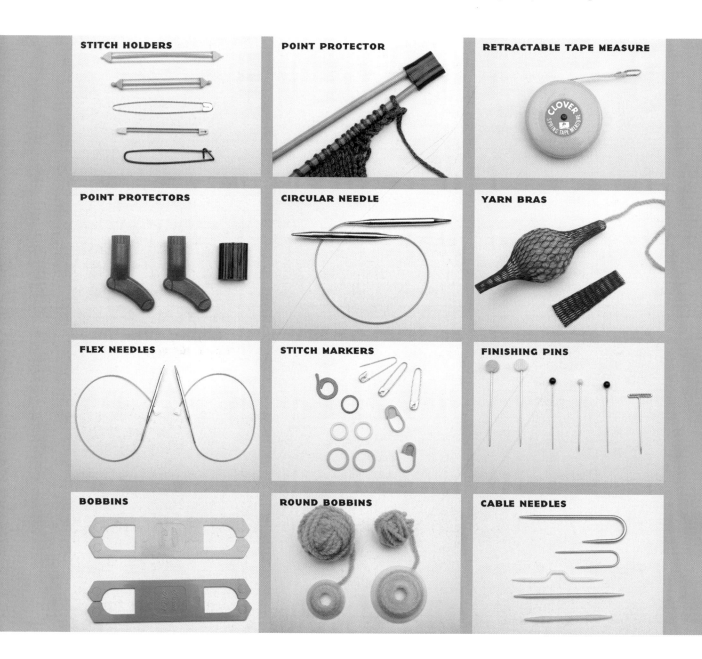

STITCH HOLDERS

POINT PROTECTOR

RETRACTABLE TAPE MEASURE

POINT PROTECTORS

CIRCULAR NEEDLE

YARN BRAS

FLEX NEEDLES

STITCH MARKERS

FINISHING PINS

BOBBINS

ROUND BOBBINS

CABLE NEEDLES

clicker-style hand counter to the one you place at the end of the needle (which can often turn by itself and cause a miscount and confusion in the pattern). And last but not least, I recommend purchasing a knitting bag to carry your projects. It's fun to accessorize and make a knitting fashion statement: that's why we carry some terrific custom-made knitting bags in a variety of stylish shapes, sizes, and fabrics, each made with multiple pockets for needles and accessories.

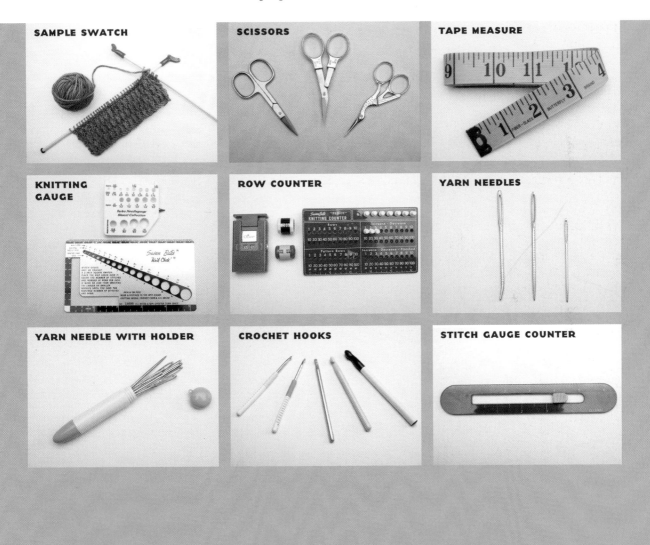

SAMPLE SWATCH

SCISSORS

TAPE MEASURE

KNITTING GAUGE

ROW COUNTER

YARN NEEDLES

YARN NEEDLE WITH HOLDER

CROCHET HOOKS

STITCH GAUGE COUNTER

Your First Pattern.
New knitters generally need some guidance when selecting their first project. Often, new mothers are eager to knit a baby blanket, though as a rule I recommend beginning with a straight piece, like a scarf. Scarves knit up quickly and give you the satisfaction of completing a project. This simple project also gives you a chance to develop tension control, the ability to knit smooth, even stitches that are uniform in size and appearance. Until you have developed tension control, a blanket would be so irregular in dimension—"pulling in and pulling out"—that you would be unhappy with the results. On a scarf the same effect can look as if it is part of the pattern.

LET'S KNIT

We have a motto at La Knitterie Parisienne: "As ye shall knit, so shall ye rip." Regardless of your knitting ability, every knitter—beginner and experienced alike—will rip their work at one point or another. If you're going to learn to knit, you need to be prepared to rip and start again. No one is exempt from ripping; even I have to do it quite frequently.

Casting On: The Two-Ball Method.
Casting on is the process of creating the first row of stitches. There are many ways to cast on, but the one I find most effective is the two-ball method. It is simple and easy (and also the fastest). This technique of casting on guarantees that you will never run out of yarn. I developed this approach years ago when I needed to cast on 400 stitches for a blanket—and ran out of yarn at 382 stitches. Necessity, after all, is the mother of invention.

Read your pattern and see how many stitches you need to cast on.

STEP 1: Pull out a length of yarn from ball #1, approximately an eight-inch tail or enough to wrap around your thumb.

STEP 2: Wrap your yarn around your left thumb with your thumb sticking up as if you were going to hitchhike and insert the needle through the loop.

STEP 3: With the tail of ball #2 in your right hand, bring the yarn counterclockwise between the needle and your left thumb.

STEP 4: With your right hand, take your yarn counterclockwise from the tail of ball #2 and place it between the needle and your thumb. Take the loop that is on your left thumb and bring it over the tip of the needle in your right hand.

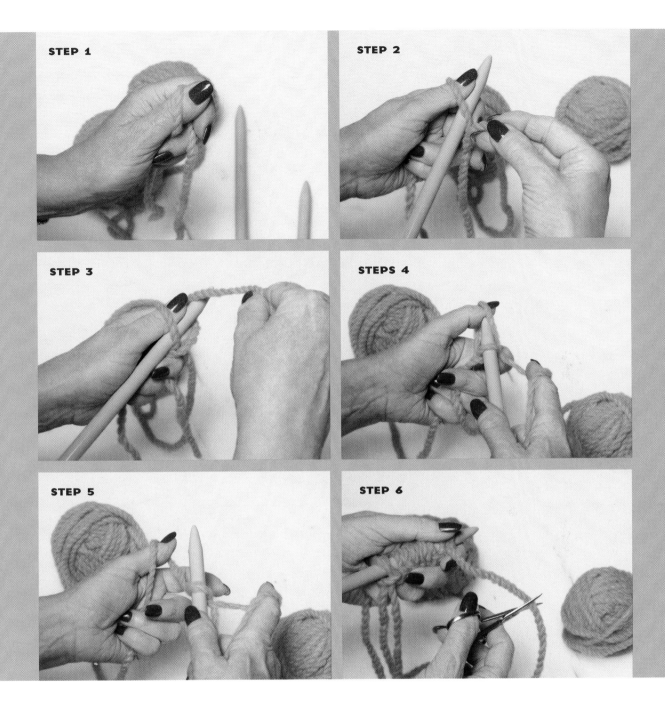

STEP 1

STEP 2

STEP 3

STEPS 4

STEP 5

STEP 6

STEP 5: With your right hand, gently pull on the tail of the ball to firm up your stitch. Avoid pulling too tightly. Your stitches should be able to gently glide along the needle.

STEP 6: Continue with this method until you have cast on the desired number of stitches. At this point you can cut either one of the two balls. Once you master this technique, you will notice that you are basically knitting using your thumb as the second needle.

Knit with the Needle, Not with the Tip

It's important to remember that when knitting to always keep the stitches past the tip of the right-hand needle. The stitches, however, can remain very close to the tip on the left-hand needle for easy removal. Always keep a finger from your left hand on the first stitch to prevent it from slipping off. Remember, the tip of the needle is only used as a guide and is not the same size as the rest of the needle. If you keep the stitches on the tip of the right-hand needle and don't slide them along the needle as you knit, your stitches will become too tight and impossible to knit with.

Knitting consists of two basic stitches: the knit stitch and the purl stitch. Once these are mastered, any project can be accomplished regardless of difficulty. Virtually every pattern created is a combination of the knit and the purl stitch. The knit stitch is the foundation of knitting, and it is important to do it well before you proceed to its companion, the purl stitch.

Learning how to knit is a simple four-step process, which can be easily remembered with a knitting verse that I originally created for children. It helps in visualizing the cast-on process. First, cast on approximately 20 stitches for practicing. Once you've accomplished this, follow these four steps: (1) go up the front door, (2) around the tree, (3) down the cellar, and (4) off you go.

STEP 1: *Go up the Front Door:* Hold the needle with your stitches on it in your left hand, and slip the tip of the right needle through the front loop, from the bottom up, holding the yarn attached to the ball in your right hand. You'll want to maintain a constant tension; your yarn should be firmly taut but not tight. Wrap the yarn from the ball around your right index finger, holding the yarn firmly in the palm of your hand. Your needles now form an X.

Keep Count of Your Stitches

One of the most frustrating things about knitting is the endless counting of stitches, especially when you have a large number of them. To make this task easier, I suggest placing a stitch marker every 20 stitches and using the markers to count and keep track of your cast-ons.

STEP 2: *Around the Tree:* With the right-hand needle underneath the left-hand needle, move the yarn around from behind the needle, toward the front in a counterclockwise motion through the X. Maintain a constant tension between your right hand and the strand of yarn. Bring the yarn behind the right needle, then pull it toward you between the X.

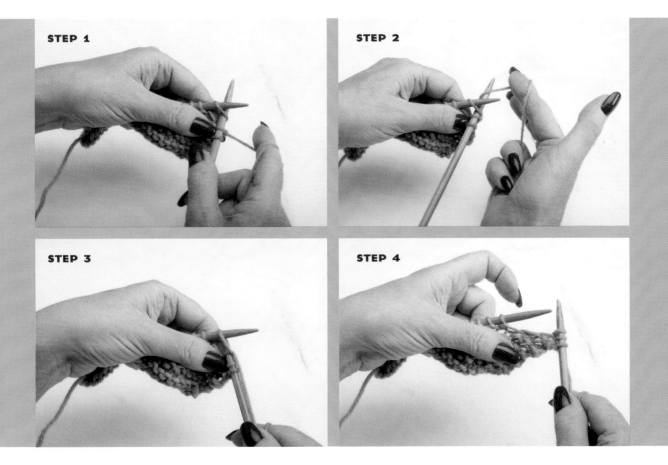

STEP 3: *Down the Cellar:* In a downward motion, gently pull the right-hand needle back through the loop that is still attached to your left-hand needle.

STEP 4: *And off You Go:* With your right-hand needle, gently pull the stitch off the left-hand needle, carefully avoiding accidentally pulling other stitches off the left-hand needle.

Congratulations! You have just knitted your first stitch.

MEGAN MULLALLY

An artist at heart, Megan would spend hours wandering the shop searching for all the right yarns—not just the right yarn, because every project of Megan's was an intricate mix of yarns: thick and thin and all color shades. From scarves to ponchos, her pieces were unusual and beautiful.

Tension. By maintaining consistent tension in your knitting, you will create even and uniform stitches as you pass them from one needle to the other.

Purling. The purl stitch is basically the reverse of the knit stitch. Follow these easy steps to master the purl stitch.

STEP 1: With your yarn in front of the right-hand needle, insert the tip of the right-hand needle through the loop, from the top downward. You've now formed an X.

STEP 2: With your right hand, take the yarn and place it over the top of the right-hand needle in a counterclockwise motion through the X.

STEP 3: Place the right-hand needle beneath the stitch on the left-hand needle and pull the yarn through the loop.

STEP 4: Pull off the stitch. Congratulations, you've just purled.

[EDITH **KNIT TIP**]

Recognizing a Knit Stitch from a Purl Stitch

Working in combination of knit one row, purl one row is referred to as stockinette. Knitting every row is called the garter stitch. Here's an easy way to recognize your stitches. When you work in stockinette, you knit the front of your work, which will be smooth; each stitch will look like a V. This side is also referred to as the "right side." On the reverse side, or "wrong side," you will purl; this row will form a series of little bumps like beads or "pearls." (The one exception is the garter stitch, which forms little bumps on both sides of the work, regardless of knitting or purling each row. This will also help you to recognize the "right" and "wrong" sides of the cast-on edge.)

I have many clients who have knitted for years and are still intimidated by the purl stitch, professing that they will learn it "next week." It may take someone years before they finally attempt it. Purling may feel awkward, but it's very simple. Once you learn to purl, and feel comfortable with the stitch, you will be able to develop your skills beyond that "professional beginner" giveaway: the knit stitch scarf, commonly referred to as the garter stitch.

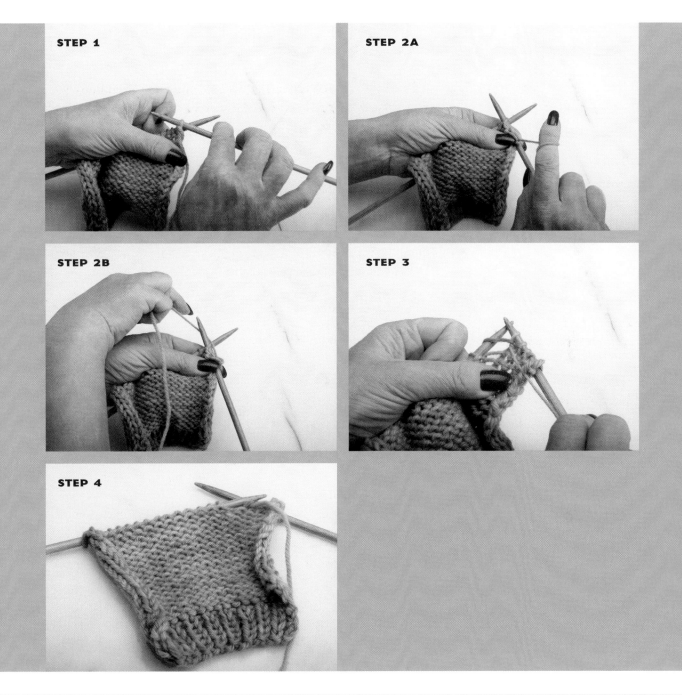

STEP 1

STEP 2A

STEP 2B

STEP 3

STEP 4

PURLING PROBLEMS

If you find purling difficult, take comfort in the fact that many of my celebrity clients have been just as puzzled by it. One of my favorite knitters is Sofia Coppola. She came in one afternoon, and I taught her how to knit, and because she was ambitious we covered purling as well. She purchased her yarn and left. A few days later I received a frantic phone call: it was Sofia, on the beach in Jamaica—with her knitting in a tangle on her lap. She had forgotten how to purl. I talked her through the stitch on the phone, and after half an hour she hung up. She finished her scarf and it was lovely.

Bind Off Loosely

When binding off, be sure to do so loosely; otherwise you risk "puckering" your work. I often recommend to my clients that they bind off using a needle one size larger than the one they've been knitting with.

Watch Out for Knots and Adding a Ball of Yarn

On occasion, you may find a knot in your yarn as you knit. It's important not to continue knitting at this point, working the knot into the row, because the knot may open, resulting in a hole in your work, or it may appear on the "right" side of your work. Instead, undo your stitches to the beginning of the row, open the knot, and attach the two ends with a slipknot, leaving a minimum of six inches that you will weave into your work later on as part of the finishing. Don't assume that expensive yarn won't have a knot in it. Even giants have feet of clay.

When adding a new ball of yarn to your work, the same rule applies: attach with a slipknot at the end of the row, leaving a six-inch tail to weave in later.

When you start to purl, everything feels upside down. The most important thing to remember is that you throw your yarn toward the floor rather than up and around.

Before you cast on for your first project, practice knitting and purling. The more relaxed and confident you are, the better you will knit.

Binding Off.
Last, but not least, is the final essential: binding off. Binding off is the process of ending and securing your work by interlocking your stitches to prevent them from unraveling and running. It is also used to shape your work, including necks and armholes.

Before you bind off your stitches, look at the cast-on row of your knitting, which is the first bottom row, to determine the "right" and "wrong" side of your knitting.

STEP 1: As you bind off, work the first two stitches in pattern.

STEP 2: You will now have two stitches on your right-hand needle.

STEP 3: Using the tip of the left-hand needle, pass the first stitch over the second stitch, letting it drop off the right-hand needle.

STEP 4: Continue working in this fashion until you've completed the row.

STEP 5: When you have one final stitch remaining on your right-hand needle, cut your yarn, leaving a six-inch tail.

STEP 6: Pull the tail through the loop of the stitch to secure it.

When working in pattern, make sure to bind off in the same pattern as this will ensure continuity and elasticity in your work.

STEP 1

STEP 2

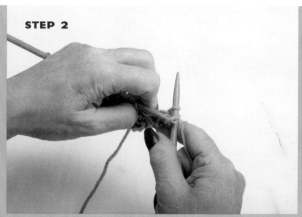

STEP 3

STEP 4

STEP 5

STEP 6

DROPPED STITCHES

While you're working on your project, you may notice what appears to be a "run" in your knitting—a loop of a stitch sticking out from the body of your work. Above this stitch you'll notice little bars, like rungs on a ladder. It's important to prevent the stitch(es) from running farther down your work and potentially ruining your project. (If you are unable to deal with the stitch immediately, secure it with a safety pin to stop it from running.) As swiftly as possible, catch the loop with either your needle or a crochet hook. Don't panic. No matter how bad it may look, or how far down in your knitting it has run, in most instances it can be repaired. You'll now begin the process of picking up your dropped stitch(es). Essentially you will be reknitting your fabric.

There are several ways to pick up a dropped stitch, and here are a few suggestions. Some people use a crochet hook to weave the loop up, but I, however, find my knitting needles to be a much more efficient way of doing this because you are applying the same techniques and motions as in knitting.

[EDITH **KNIT TIP**]

Saving a Dropped Stitch

If you drop more than one stitch, you'll want to pick them up one at a time, after placing the other dropped stitches on a safety pin.

Picking Up a Dropped Knit Stitch

STEP 1 A—B: Insert the tip of your right-hand needle into the front of the dropped stitch.

STEP 2: With your left hand, separate the rungs of your ladder, working the rung closest to the dropped stitch first. Insert the tip of the right-hand needle under the rung.

STEP 3 A—E: Insert the tip of your left-hand needle through the stitch on the back of the stitch on your right-hand needle, pulling it through as if to bind off. Repeat this process until you've repaired your work.

STEP 1A

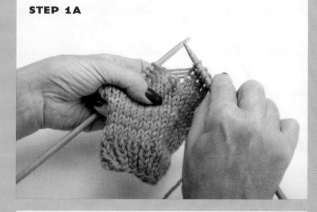

STEP 1B

STEP 2

STEP 3A

STEP 3B

STEP 3C

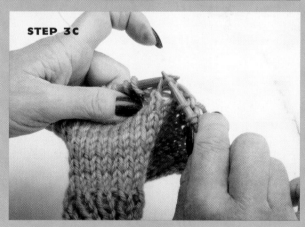

STEP 3D

STEP 3E

Picking Up a Dropped Garter Stitch. This is
why as I mentioned earlier, it's important to be able to recognize your knit and purl stitches.

STEP 1: Even though for a garter stitch you knit every row, the ridge formed by doing so consists of a combination of knit and purl. If you look carefully at your ridge, you'll see the bottom line forming a "V" while the top part looks like a purl. The first step is to look at the first rung and to recognize if the stitch dropped from the knit or the purl ridge. Place the dropped stitch on your left-hand needle. Insert the tip of the right-hand needle into the stitch as if to purl and at the same time, under the rung, pulling it through. The stitch is picked up. Resume your work.

[EDITH **KNIT TIPS**]

Saving a Dropped Stitch— with a Twist

Picking up a dropped stitch on the purl side is easy. Simply turn your work so that the knit side is facing you and follow the process on page 11.

RIPPING OUT YOUR WORK

There is nothing worse than looking at your knitting and realizing you have made a "big" mistake. Maybe you knitted where you should have purled, neglected to increase, or just knitted a piece longer than it needed to be. In any case, you are going to have to undo or rip out your knitting to the point where you made your mistake, fix the error, and continue forward. More than any other aspect of knitting, ripping is frustrating and annoying.

SOFIA COPPOLA

Because Sofia loved knitting so much, she wanted to be able to incorporate it into her film Lost in Translation. *So she asked me*

to design an original pattern and knit a scarf for the film's lead female character, Charlotte, played by Scarlett Johansson.

The powder blue cashmere scarf is featured prominently in the Academy Award–winning film and also featured in this book.

One of my first forays into the world of Hollywood knitting took place shortly after I opened my shop. I was approached to teach the cast of Theresa Rebeck's Loose Knit *theatrical production how to knit. The story centered around five contemporary New York City women of diverse backgrounds who gathered to form a knitting group. It was particularly important for each member of the acting troupe to be able to knit proficiently since the loosely knit threads that bring the women to-gether are eventually woven into a tight fabric of friendship and family. I took on the role of knitting coach and worked diligently with the group, teaching them to knit for over five months. On opening night, I was thrilled to see that I was credited as the knitting coach in the* Playbill.

During the months of coaching, the entire cast would come to the shop on a weekly basis to practice. Midway through the lessons, Daryl Hannah came to

the shop to learn to knit, and loved the informal knitting circle so much that she too decided to become a part of the in-store Loose Knit *knitting circle.*

Preventing Dropped Stitches

One common problem knitters have when working with big needles and bulky yarn is that the yarn often slips off the head of the needle because the loops tend to be larger than the cap of the needle. To prevent this from happening, cut two disks out of cardboard, make a hole in the center the size of your needle, and slide it toward the cap of the needle before you start your work. You'll be amazed at how this simple trick will protect the stitches from falling off.

Size Matters

Before you insert your needle into the row of ripped stitches, here's a good tip to make this process easier. I recommend using a needle several sizes smaller than the one you are using. Since the left-hand needle functions as a stitch holder, the smaller needle won't affect your knitting for this row, but you must remember to replace it with your original needle when you begin the next row.

There are two ways to go backward in your knitting. One is simply "unknitting," or reversing the knitting or purling action so that instead of moving your yarn from the left needle to the right needle and adding a stitch, you are moving the yarn from the right needle to the left and removing a stitch. To do this, insert the tip of your left needle into the stitch *under* the stitch on your right needle. Pull the stitch off the right needle and gently pull at the yarn. Your stitch will slip through the loop of the stitch that is now sitting on your left needle. Continue as necessary.

Ripping Out an Entire Sweater

Sometimes all you can do is admit that your sweater just isn't going to work: you made a bad color choice, or it's too small or just too unflattering. You'll have to rip the whole thing, but what to do with all those loose yards of yarn? I tell my knitters to wrap the yarn around the back of a chair as they rip it—wrapping it firmly, but being careful not to stretch it. You'll notice the yarn has tons of little kinks in it. To eliminate these kinks, spray the yarn with cold water and then let it dry while keeping it on the back of the chair. Make sure the yarn is completely dry before rolling it into a ball.

Beginning with Garter

For beginner knitters, I recommend knitting the typical beginner scarf in the garter stitch. First, because it's much easier, and second, because the edges of the scarf—unlike if knitted in stockinette, which will roll—will remain flat.

The second is more involved and mainly used if you've made a major error and need to undo more than one or two rows in your knitting. When this happens, you'll have to rip. First, determine how far down you'll need to rip, and identify the row by placing a safety pin in the center of it. Lay your work down on a flat surface and simply remove the needle. Next, slowly and gently pull the strand of yarn to undo the stitches, working one row at a time until you reach the safety pin. Now replace the stitches on the needle and continue your work.

After you've picked up your row and resumed knitting, you may notice that some of the stitches are backward. You'll be able to recognize this as it will be difficult to knit or purl. When this happens, simply insert your right-hand needle through the back loop of the stitch and knit it. The stitch will automatically right itself.

So far, you've grasped the basics of knitting, learned to bind off, and even how to rip. But more important, I hope you're having fun in the process. Knitting is an enjoyable and creative outlet, so enjoy the ride.

KNITTING FOR FILMS

Although I have knitted quite a lot of projects for films over the years, from Christmas stockings for Jamie Lee Curtis in Christmas with the Kranks, *to the scarf for Scarlett Johansson in* Lost in Translation, *to slippers for Sissy Spacek in* Blast from the Past, *to name a few— I declined an offer to knit for a* Budweiser commercial in which they wanted me to make sweaters for rats.

chapter two

THE NEXT STEP

If you want beautiful, sophisticated knitting, there is no way around the fact that you need to learn how to make and use a knitted gauge. Of course, this doesn't stop people from trying to figure out a way to avoid having to do it. When I informed one new knitter that she would need a gauge, she replied, "Fine, where do I buy one?"

It's 8:00 p.m. on a typical Wednesday and La Knitterie Parisienne is filled with eager knitters. Wednesday is late night, when the many knitters who can't get away during the day come to knit among friends in the evening. We have a real mix of people here: aspiring actresses sit next to Oscar winners; studio executives gratefully accept help from assistants. At any point during the day or evening, we may have as many as forty to fifty people crowded in the shop, sitting around the large wooden table, crouching on the floor, all strangers to one another, talking, laughing, and enjoying each other's company.

Nonknitters might be surprised at how passionate and loud the talk grows by the end of the night. During the last election the conversations got so heated, we took a poll and elected to ban any talk of politics—but that's what I love about Wednesday nights: it's a real family, with all the emotions and energy that a family has.

On any given day, there may be as many as twenty knitters gathered around the table, all of whom patiently await my help. And since I have yet to master the ability to clone myself, one of the best things about the knitting circle is how my clients assist each other until I can make my way to them. While it's the more proficient knitters who guide beginners, everyone offers an opinion, advice, and comfort. It's satisfying to see how my clients truly care about knitting and offer encouragement. After all, if you see someone who has only been knitting for six months manage to shape a sweater or master cabling, then you'll be inspired to advance your skills as well.

As I tell my clients, it's important to choose your next project with an increased level of difficulty so you're continuously challenging yourself and improving your knitting skills.

STAR SIGHTINGS

Since La Knitterie Parisienne opened its doors in 1996, we've enjoyed the reputation as a haven where the famous and the nonfamous gather, sharing at least one thing in common: their love of knitting. And, while it's well-known that celebrities have helped to catapult knitting's popularity, the celebrities aren't always immediately recognizable. For instance, not too long ago, I had two new knitters sitting next to each other; the first was a stay-at-home mom, the second a beautiful brunette— who also happened to be an Academy Award–winning actress. As they knitted, I overheard the first woman whisper to the second, "I'm kind of disappointed, I was hoping to see a movie star, but it's just regular people tonight." With a completely straight face, the leading lady whispered back to her, "I know, I'm disappointed too!"

I remember opening People *magazine one day and seeing Sarah Jessica and Kristin sitting in director's chairs on the set of* Sex and the City, *knitting. I had to chuckle. They were knitting with the yarn I had just sent to them. Another time, Sarah Jessica called me requesting a particular yarn that she said she couldn't find anywhere in New York after searching several knitting shops. When* Sex and the City *wrapped production, I designed and knit both Sarah Jessica and Kristin what I envisioned to be the quintessential "Sex and the City Scarf" (the pattern is featured in my book). They both called to say thank you; I was glad to hear the scarf was a hit. Kristin has since moved back to Los Angeles, and I'm delighted to be able to see her more frequently.*

Now that you've learned the basics—casting on, binding off, knitting, and purling—you're ready to graduate to the next three essential steps. Remember that knitting is based on two basic stitches: the knit and the purl stitch, and in combination, you can create virtually any pattern imaginable. With the addition of tension control, ribbing, and shaping to your repertoire, you are on your way to becoming an expert knitter. Without these skills your knitting would be limited to shapeless, flat pieces. Don't be disheartened if they seem difficult at first. Like with everything else, practice makes perfect.

TENSION AND GAUGE

Every master has her tools. In addition to my yarn and needles, I'm never without the telephone by my side, the tape measure dangling around my neck, and my signature red manicured nails. True, you might not need two of the three, but you will always need a tape measure—to measure your project and, in this case, to measure your gauge as you knit with the proper tension.

What Is Tension? The first thing you need to master is tension: the way in which you hold your yarn as you knit. As in the classic story of the "Three Bears," it's important to hold your yarn "just right." If you hold the yarn too loosely, your stitches will be too large and holey; if you pull your yarn too tight, your stitches will be tight and difficult to move along the needle.

I recently helped a woman rip out a scarf that was so wide it looked like the back of a coat; she was annoyed and couldn't understand how this could have happened. After all, she'd already knitted several scarves, and just as before she had cast on 18 stitches. The one thing she failed to understand was that rather than the medium weight yarn she had used in the past, she had selected a very bulky yarn for this project. Instead of ending up with 5 stitches to an inch she had 2, and thus her project was considerably wider—and unwearable. There is a simple solution to this problem: knitting a gauge. Had she taken the time to work up a gauge, she would have had a perfect blueprint of her finished scarf.

What Is a Gauge?

A gauge—also referred to as a swatch—is the *most* critical part of knitting because it is the recommended number of stitches and rows per inch required to successfully knit your project to size. For instance, if a pattern calls for 5 stitches and 6 rows per inch, you would make your gauge by casting on 20 stitches and working for 24 rows. A sample of your work for your project—or the gauge—should be a 4-by-4-inch swatch. The needles recommended in the pattern is just that: a recommendation. If you are a tight knitter, you may have to go up one or more needle sizes, and if you are a loose knitter, you may have to go down several needles sizes. It might take you up to half an hour to knit a gauge, but it will also save you countless hours of frustration. Be sure to always knit your gauge in the stitch stipulated in the pattern.

A lot of new knitters are unwilling to learn the technical aspects of knitting. They come to the store and ask me, "How many stitches do I need to cast on?" My standard response is that I forgot my crystal ball at home. Without knowing how many stitches they get to an inch, there's no way to answer their question. I find that 90 percent of the people are willing to knit a gauge, while just 10 percent will shrug their shoulders. It's these few who come back with ill-fitting garments, even though they claim to have followed the directions in the pattern. Here are a few guidelines you can follow before beginning to knit to ensure you'll obtain the right gauge.

[EDITH KNIT TIP]

Your Mood Will Affect Your Gauge

Never knit a gauge when you are angry or stressed. This will affect how you knit and ultimately the size of your gauge.

Measuring Your Work

When you measure your work, make sure that the piece is completely flat. If need be, you may have to take some stitches off the needles to ensure there is no bunching as this will cause the garment to appear longer than it really is.

- Try to use the yarn recommended in your pattern. If you want to substitute another yarn, make sure that the gauge indicated on the label is the same as the one described in the pattern. Ask your local knitting store for guidance if necessary. If the original yarn is available, compare your substitute to it. Read the labels to ensure they have the same characteristics: same stitch and row gauge.

- Read the yarn label carefully when selecting your needles as you will need to distinguish between European and U.S. sizes. European measurements will be given in metrics and will need to be converted to U.S. sizing. Labels will also list two sizes of needles with the first always two sizes smaller than the second. This is *not* a range of needles to be used. Rather, the first is the recommended size for the ribbing. The second, larger needle is the one to be used for the body of the garment.

- Each pattern will indicate exactly what stitch and how many stitches to cast on to create a 4-by-4-inch swatch. When measuring the gauge, it is essential to measure the entire 4-inch width to get an accurate reading of both the number of stitches per inch as well as the number of rows per inch. If you cheat and measure only over a few stitches, you will not get an accurate measurement.

- If you don't achieve your gauge with the recommended needle size, you can rectify this by adjusting the needle size, either going up or down a size. Remember to alter the size of the needle you use to work your rib.

You're on your way. Soon enough you'll be ready to tackle your first knitted garment.

RIBBING

Ribbing is an essential part of the knitting process. In its most common form, ribbing is used to shape a garment, from hats to gloves to sweaters, and to create elasticity at the base of the sweater, cuffs, and neck. Although there are numerous patterns to create ribbing, the most common is the knit one, purl one rib.

The key to mastering ribbing is to understand the way you move the yarn from the front to the back of your work, between the needles. To help my clients visualize and remember this basic two-step process, I use this image: Imagine that your needles form the posts of a door. You must move the yarn through the posts (or needles), not over them, before inserting the needle into the stitch. This will ensure that you don't inadvertently create extra stitches.

STEP 1: For example, in the knit one, purl one (K1, P1) rib, if your first stitch is a knit, bring your yarn to the back of your work and knit as usual.

STEP 2: The next step will be a purl stitch; bring your yarn forward to the front of your work and purl the second stitch.

STEP 3–6: Make sure that you are bringing the yarn *through the door,* not wrapping it over or behind the needles—the yarn should just be going back and forward between the needles without touching them. Simple, isn't it? Now continue this pattern across the row.

There are a few obvious mistakes that can be made when knitting a rib, the most serious being when the knitter forgets which stitch to knit and which stitch to purl and gets "out of synch," creating a row of seed stitches rather than ribbing. If this happens, the only solution is to rip. As long as you remember to purl the purl stitches and knit the knit stitches, you will be okay.

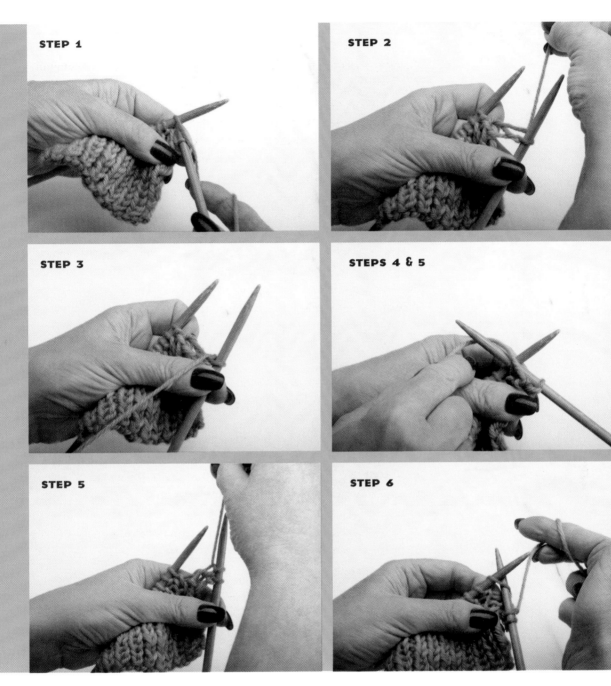

STEP 1

STEP 2

STEP 3

STEPS 4 & 5

STEP 5

STEP 6

Changing Color While Ribbing

When changing colors within your ribbing, always start by knitting across the row and then rib on the wrong side. This will help to avoid seeing a line of color on the front of your work.

BASIC SHAPING

The next skill we are going to learn in this chapter is how to add shape to your knitting with increases and decreases. After all, how are you going to knit a sweater if you don't know how to make it fit?

When you knit an increase, it widens your piece of knitting by one stitch, so by alternating rows with increases and rows without increases, you get a gradual widening that follows the shape of the body from the waist up toward the shoulders. Decreases do the opposite: they narrow your knitting.

There are several ways to increase and decrease, but for now we will cover the most basic and easiest technique.

Increasing. There are numerous ways to increase the number of stitches in your knitting. Increasing is usually done at the edges of your work. Here are the three most commonly used techniques:

METHOD A: Step 1A & Step 1B Knit the stitch without removing the loop from the left-hand needle, Step 2 insert the needle into the back of the same stitch, knit it, and Step 3 remove the stitch from the needle.

METHOD B: Step 1 Insert your needle into the stitch from the row below and twist it onto your left-hand needle; Step 2 knit that stitch and Step 3A/3B immediately knit the following stitch on the needle. I prefer this technique because it creates a smooth and even surface and won't cause a noticeable disruption in the look of your knitting.

METHOD C: The third way to increase is commonly called a "make one." The advantage to this method is that it can be made anywhere across the row without distorting the look of your work, whereas the two methods previously discussed should only be used at the beginning or end of a row. To create a make one, knit across the row to the point where you want to

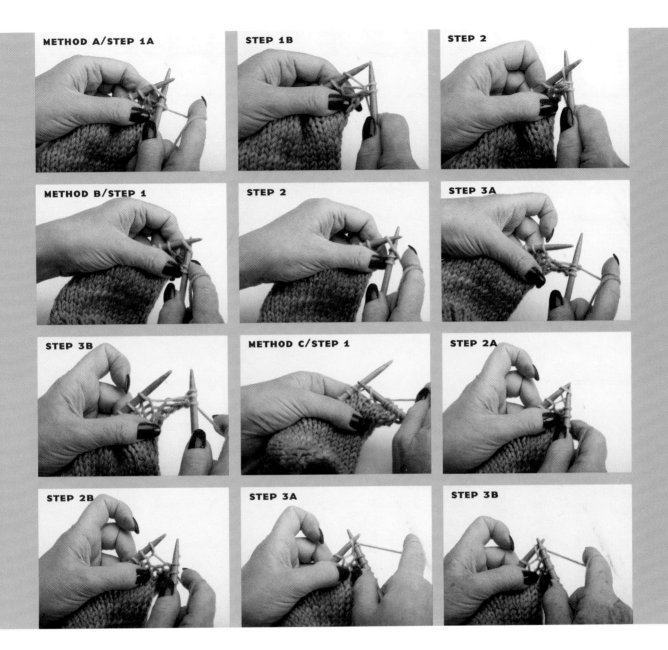

METHOD A/STEP 1A

STEP 1B

STEP 2

METHOD B/STEP 1

STEP 2

STEP 3A

STEP 3B

METHOD C/STEP 1

STEP 2A

STEP 2B

STEP 3A

STEP 3B

increase. Look at the knitting between the stitch on your left-hand needle and the stitch on your right-hand needle; you'll clearly see a "bar." Step 1, with your right-hand needle, pick the bar from behind and Step 2A transfer to left-hand needle, Step 2B then Step 3A/3B, insert the point of your right-hand needle through the back loop and knit it.

Decreasing. There are several methods of decreasing, the goal of which is to eliminate one or more stitches from your work. The most important thing about decreasing is that you need to change your method depending on where you need to decrease in your knitting. This is because decreasing affects the look of your knitting and is directional. If you use decreases correctly, they can add a polished look to your work. Use them incorrectly and they will be ugly and obvious. Choose your decrease technique based on whether you are working on the left or right side of your work.

- Knit two together (K2tog): This is the easiest way to decrease, and the decrease will slant to the right.

- Purl two together (P2tog): Insert the right-hand needle through the next two stitches and purl them together.

- Slip one, knit one, pass slipped stitch over (SL1, K1, PSSO): Slip a stitch as if to purl (or purlwise), knit the next stitch, and pass the slipped stitch over the previously knitted stitch. The decrease will slant to the left.

- Binding off as a method of decreasing: I'm often asked, "Why do I bind off instead of decreasing?" The difference is that binding off is eliminating more than one consecutive stitch and can only be done at the beginning of a row. For example, when shaping the armhole of a sweater, you will bind off at the beginning of a knit row for the right armhole and at the beginning of the purl row for the left armhole. Even though a decrease of a single stitch is generally done at the beginning of a row, it can also be used anywhere throughout the row.

- Full fashion decreases: This means that the decreases on the armholes and sleeves have been knitted in such a way that they become a design feature, outlining the shaping of the separate pieces of knitting. To do this you will generally want to work your decreases only on the knit rows, and work all decreases two stitches in from the edge of your knitting. On the right side you will use K2tog, and on the left side you will use the slip one, knit one, pass slipped stitch over method.

K2 TOG

K2 TOG

K2 TOG

SL1, K1, PSSO

SL1, K1, PSSO

SL1, K1, PSSO

SL1, K1, PSSO

SL1, K1, PSSO

Using a Cable Needle Correctly

If you use a hook cable needle, make sure to remove the stitches from the left-hand needle with the short side and knit the stitches from the left-hand needle with the long side. By doing this, the stitches will automatically be twisted and face the correct direction.

CABLING

One technique that scares people the most is cabling. Well, you need not be frightened as this is one of the easiest of all to master. In a pattern a simple cable is very often referred to as a "4-stitch cable," "6-stitch cable," or "12-stitch cable." This indicates how many stitches will be involved in the cable process. When cabling, you will also need a spare needle, called an auxiliary or cable needle, a needle that has a bend or hook feature.

Here's an example of how to cable. Let's say that the pattern calls for a 6-stitch cable. To make a "back cable," which will form a slant to the right, follow this simple step:

With the tip of your cable needle, remove 3 stitches from your left-hand needle and let them rest in the curve of your cable needle; place them in the back of your work. Knit the 3 stitches on your left-hand needle, then knit the 3 from your cable needle. The cable is made.

To make a "front cable," or left twist. Slip 3 stitches onto a cable needle and place it to the front of your work. Knit the 3 stitches from the left-hand needle, then knit the 3 from the cable needle. You have now mastered the art of cabling.

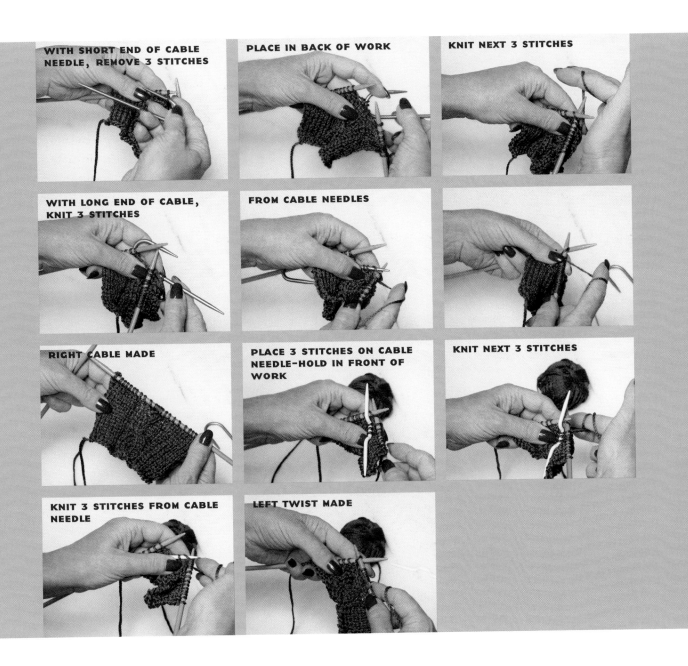

WITH SHORT END OF CABLE NEEDLE, REMOVE 3 STITCHES

PLACE IN BACK OF WORK

KNIT NEXT 3 STITCHES

WITH LONG END OF CABLE, KNIT 3 STITCHES

FROM CABLE NEEDLES

RIGHT CABLE MADE

PLACE 3 STITCHES ON CABLE NEEDLE—HOLD IN FRONT OF WORK

KNIT NEXT 3 STITCHES

KNIT 3 STITCHES FROM CABLE NEEDLE

LEFT TWIST MADE

CABLE CAST ON

As you are knitting a sweater or a garment made in one piece, the instructions will indicate "cable cast on X stitches." This is accomplished by adding stitches at the beginning of the row while your work is in progress. To do so, proceed as follows:

STEP 1: Insert your right-hand needle between the first and second stitches on the left-hand needle.

STEP 2: Pull up a loop.

STEP 3: Insert your left-hand needle under the loop that has been placed on the right-hand needle, then release it from the right-hand needle. Continue in this manner until you have cable cast on the number of stitches recommended in your pattern.

There are four simple skills that a knitter needs to master in order to consider themselves a proficient knitter: knitting, purling, increasing, and decreasing. I hope that after reading chapters one and two, you will feel confident enough to practice and apply these skills in your own work. Once you have done so, you will find that knitting is an open door, and that if you understand the basics, you can learn to incorporate new stitches, techniques, and ideas in your projects.

[EDITH **KNIT TIPS**]

Flash Cards

When cabling or following a difficult pattern, here's an easy way to keep track of your rows. Write each row on its own flash card and flip the cards as you finish each row.

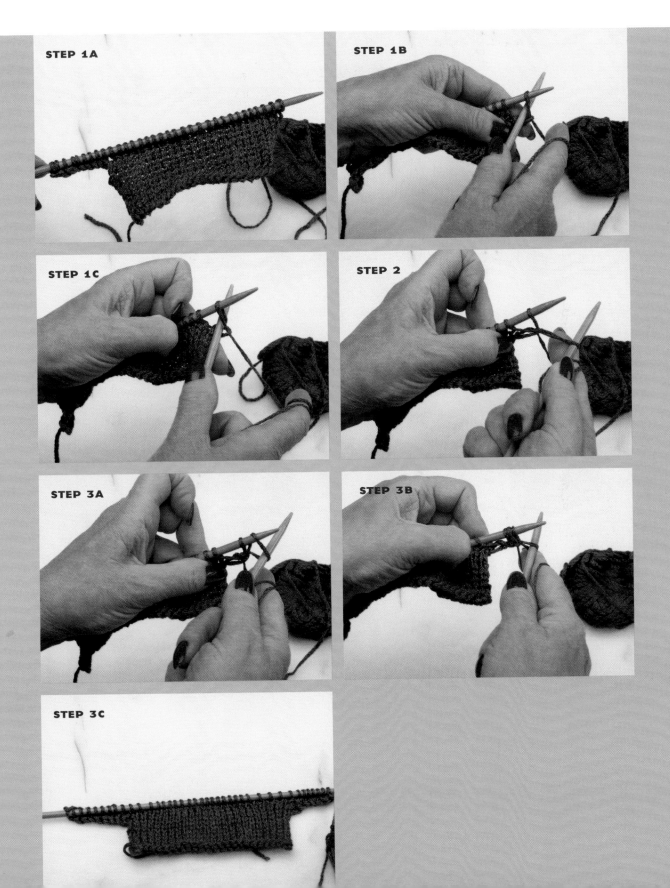

STEP 1A

STEP 1B

STEP 1C

STEP 2

STEP 3A

STEP 3B

STEP 3C

Don't be afraid of your knitting and don't be afraid to try something new. I had one knitter who was working on a sweater made with an even number of stitches. She finished the back, but when it came time to do the front she decided she wanted a V-neck instead of the crewneck I had originally designed for her. V-necks need an odd number of stitches in order to create the neckline. So I said, "Continue your ribbing on an even number of stitches, but when you knit the body of your sweater increase it by one stitch." When I told her this she started to panic, because it didn't make sense to her that adding one stitch at the side of her knitting could possibly be okay. In the end she reverted back to her original plan and made it the crewneck. Please don't be scared of your knitting. If it doesn't work, you can always rip, but, more important, you will never become a better, more skillful knitter if you are afraid to take risks with your knitting.

Hilary Shephard

chapter three

EXPLORING YARNS

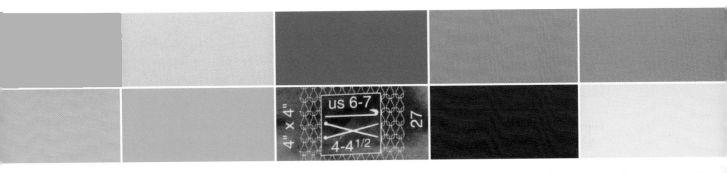

There is a joke about two ladies who died and went
to heaven and found a room full of yarn—but no
needles. Who knows, maybe it wasn't heaven
after all. . . .

Working with Leftover Yarn

Ever wonder what to do with that stash of yarns from other projects? Here's a fun idea that I share with my clients and even do myself: try knitting a poncho, a scarf, a hat, or a blanket in a striped pattern.

Blending Dye Lots

When you're working on a project and you find you're running out of yarn and the dye lot is no longer available, try this. Unravel some of the previous work and gradually add the new yarn, alternating two rows of one dye lot with the other to blend the two together.

I believe that quality materials make your knitting. As soon as it is within your budget and as your skills improve, start looking at the different yarns, needles, and patterns available to you. With the basic techniques of knitting under your belt, you can now begin exploring how the vast array of yarns can suit your individual needs and also reflect your personality.

One of the most exciting aspects of knitting is how it's tailored to fit your own distinct style. While I may design the same garment for two people, the yarn they select, the stitch they choose, and the tension of the knitting will result in two completely different items, unique to each person. The concept of creating one-of-a-kind items, that can't be bought off the shelf, makes the knitting experience that much more adventurous and addicting.

JUSTINE BATEMAN

Justine came in one day because she had passed the store numerous times and decided that she wanted to learn how to knit and crochet. Justine quickly became an avid knitter, and with my help began designing her own patterns, making some unusual and rather interesting designs. They were so unique, in fact, that I suggested she sell them. The next week, she came in with a catalogue's worth of hand-knitted items: everything from hats and scarves to coats, tank tops, and dresses. She took her line, Justine Bateman Designs, to the exclusive boutique, Tracy Ross—and made her first sale, selling thirteen original pieces. I offered her some advice on how to increase her revenue for these items, and then off she went to Fred Segal's, where she sold fifteen Justine Bateman Design coats. One of the most sincere people I've met, Justine has never lost sight of the whole knitting experience, always crediting me with teaching and guiding her along the way. Justine has become a good friend of mine, and I was thrilled to be able to attend her wedding and baby showers.

Patricia had something extremely unusual in mind to | *knit: drapes. She came in and bought a selection of green yarns* | *to make drapes.*

The great thing about knitting is that it is an inherently logical craft. With clear directions, and an understanding of the basic concepts, you can accomplish any kind of tricky stitch or complex technique.

Of the thousands of yarns I stock at La Knitterie Parisienne, nearly all are made of natural fibers. While my preference leans toward these types of yarns, manmade fibers combined with natural fibers can create beautiful novelty yarns. Manmade yarns have evolved in their own right, so working with them alone can also be luxurious.

Let's explore the variety of yarns available and their individual characteristics: content, texture, weight, and elasticity. Consider the yarn. Is it firm and tightly spun, or light and lofty? Does it give when you gently pull at it? Even though most yarns can be safely washed in cold water and air-dried *only*, there are some wool yarns, called superwash, that have been processed to enable you to wash them in warm water on gentle cycle and place in the dryer on low heat.

COTTON

Looks can be deceiving: not all cottons are the same. In determining quality, the most important characteristic of cotton is whether it is made up of long or short fibers. Price is one of the

[**EDITH** KNIT TIPS]

It's All in the Label

Yarn labels are a great source of information. Each label will provide the following: fiber content, yardage, gauge and needle size, color, dye lot, and washing instructions. Should you ever run out of yarn, this will ensure that you get exactly what you need with the least amount of stress—as long as you purchase the yarn in a timely manner and it's still available. If you are knitting an item for a friend, give them a label along with the gift. I always tell my clients to be sure to keep one of the labels from your project, attach a snippet of the yarn to it, and store it in a safe place. If you become a dedicated knitter, buy a knitting notebook to store all your patterns, labels, and knitting notes.

Commonsense Knitting with Cotton

When I recommend that my clients knit with cotton, I'm often met with the comment "No, cotton stretches." Since cotton has less elasticity than other fibers, it tends to lose its structure and form, giving it the illusion that it has stretched, most noticeably in ribbing. There's a remedy for this. I suggest knitting the ribbing with needles three sizes smaller than the ones with which you'll knit your garment.

key indicators of this difference. If it is inexpensive, then it's made up of short fibers (cotton that has been processed has a tendency to shed, pill, and stretch). Cottons with long virgin fibers, such as Egyptian or pima cotton, are among the finest.

Unlike your cosmetic cotton ball, which is only available in white, natural cotton grows in a variety of earth tones, including pale shades of pink, green, and beige.

Cotton is also prone to shrinking, so you'll need to account for this as you prepare to knit. That's why mercerized cottons are preferred; they've been treated with caustic soda and stretched, making them smoother and stronger and less likely to shrink and stretch.

WOOL

Wool is often used as a generic term for yarn spun from an animal. In fact, wool is only spun from the fleece of a sheep. As with cotton, you also get what you pay for with wool. Wool comes in many varieties, depending on what type of sheep it originated from. My preference is merino wool, a premium wool made from the Australian Merino sheep. It is one of the softest wools available.

Many knitters start their first project with very inexpensive yarn bought from one of the chain craft stores. It may seem like a bargain—only two or three dollars a ball—but these yarns are of inferior quality: they are

FINDING INSPIRATION

Yarns aren't the only source of inspiration for new projects. My client, Jane Lockhart of Sweet Lady Jane, the renowned baker to the stars, was inspired to knit

a cardigan. The style of the sweater was centered around a set of vintage buttons inherited from her grandmother. We had a lot fun roaming the shop until

we found the perfect yarn to enhance these vintage buttons. Inspiration is everywhere.

All Wools Are Not Created Equal

There is a clear distinction between virgin wool and pure wool. I always recommend that my clients knit with virgin wool because it comes direct from the sheep to you–unlike pure wool, which is made of recycled wool. So, to put an end to the wool controversy, wool vs. wool: unless the label specifically says "virgin wool," you are purchasing the other kind.

Ripping Mohair

Ripping out mohair can be a hairy task! Individual rows may rip quite easily, but the last stitch can keep the row tied up in knots. To make the process easier, I advise my clients to use a sharp yarn needle to pry loose the stitch and to avoid yanking to separate the strands that have become entangled.

rough to the touch and because they're held together with starch, you may notice the yarn has a sticky feel. Since you'll be investing hours in making your project, it's worth buying quality yarn that will add to the end result rather than detract from it.

I sell a broad range of wools, everything from ultrasoft fingering yarn to thicker and coarser wools that knit up into the classic ski sweater. A sturdy fabric, wool also has many practical attributes: a sheep's coat helps maintain its body temperature, keeping it warm in winter and cool in summer, all the time repelling rain and moisture. It can do the same for you—but don't forget your umbrella.

MOHAIR

Back in the '60s, every woman owned a mohair sweater. It looked stunning until you actually felt the fibers, which were rough, prickly, and itchy. Today, mohair yarns have come a long way; spun from the belly of a kid goat rather than from an adult goat, the yarn is much softer and pleasing to the touch. Mohair yarn is often misunderstood and considered to be a very thin yarn. In fact, the opposite is true: mohair is a lofty yarn because you must account for the fuzziness as well as the core when working with it.

ANGORA

Angora comes from the full underbelly of angora rabbits—not your common neighborhood bunny. Like mohair, angora is also a lofty yarn and is often mistakenly considered much thinner than it is. As a result, people tend to knit with needles that are too small, creating a tight fabric. If

Taking the Shed Out of Angora

Angora tends to shed, especially when you're working with it. Eventually, the shedding will stop on its own. To shorten this process, however, you can put the finished garment in the dryer on fluff *without any heat* (this is very important) and let it spin. As long as you're not exposing the garment to heat and high spin, you can keep the garment in the dryer on fluff for approximately a half hour. You may need to repeat this procedure several times.

you knit with needles that are too small, you risk compressing the yarn and marring the beauty of the finished product.

CASHMERE

Cashmere, one of the finest, most expensive fibers in the world, is spun from the fine, soft wool or down hair from the undercoat of a Kashmir goat. It takes one goat up to a year to produce approximately 100–150 grams of cashmere, making it one of the rarest and sought-after yarns in the world. You will need on average 350 grams, or the equivalent of three to four goats, to make a sweater.

ANGORA: SHRINKING RIGHT BEFORE YOUR VERY EYES

Years ago, people didn't account for the loftiness of angora, so they knitted the yarn with size 2 or 3 needles. One of my clients knitted a pair of angora mittens. They came out beautifully, and she wore them all the time. As spring approached, she stored them away in a drawer, carefully wrapping them in tissue paper. To her surprise—or rather horror—when she unwrapped the tissue paper, she found a pair of pelted angora mittens the size of a baby's hand. If I hadn't observed this firsthand, I wouldn't have believed it. What happened?

Well, let me tell you. While my client was wearing the mittens, her hands kept them in a stretched condition even though they wanted to shrink; however, once they were stored away, the natural heat and moisture that had been absorbed from her hands caused the angora to shrink on its own—because the mittens had been knitted with needles that were too small.

When I recounted this yarn to my angora supplier, he had an equally funny story to tell. In the 1940s at the Parisian night-club, the Folies Bergère, there was an incident involving a

woman and her angora sweater. As she sat under the show lights, sipping her wine and enjoying the performance, she began to feel a bit uncomfortable. Her sweater had begun to shrink noticeably from the heat of the lights and the moisture from her body. Apparently, as she got hotter the sweater got smaller until she finally had no choice but to leave.

It's wise to remember the properties of angora—or any fiber, for that matter: yarn continues to breathe and will react to the elements.

"Worming" in chenille can happen at any time: immediately or over a period of time. One of my clients labored over an afghan for her college-bound daughter, using several types of very expensive yarns, including chenille. When her daughter came home during Christmas break, she brought the afghan with her. My client was upset when she saw its condition: everything was smooth—except for the chenille, which was worming throughout. With my help, we undid the entire afghan, and she reworked it without the chenille. A lot of time and effort wasted.

ALPACA

Alpaca comes from the alpaca goat, a cousin of the llama and the camel and a native of South America. Alpaca is warm, soft, and luxurious to the touch. It's also significantly less expensive than cashmere and just a bit hairier. Because alpaca is very luxurious, it is commonly referred to as the poor man's cashmere.

CHENILLE

Tucked away in one of the cabinets in my shop is a pale blue sweater. When I made it some ten years ago, I was quite proud of it. I had designed a complicated pattern, including cables. As I happily began to sew the seams together, I noticed a slight looping and dismissed it as an error in my knitting. A few days later, while I was wearing it, one of my clients pointed to what appeared to be a pulled stitch. As I came to learn, these mysterious loops, also known as worming, is a negative attribute inherent to chenille. This is why I don't sell chenille in my store, despite the frequent requests I get for it. You've heard the expression "pictures are worth a thousand words"? When someone requests this yarn, I pull this garment out of hiding and show them this "worm-infested" chenille sweater—which continues to loop to this day.

ACRYLIC AND NOVELTY YARNS

Acrylic yarns come in a variety of qualities, and there are many reasons for working with them. Over the years, acrylics have evolved for the better. They are commonly found as a component in novelty yarns, including some of the more recognizable yarns as eyelash, furs, and microfibers, which have become quite popular. Acrylics are also a favorite for knitting baby blankets since they are easily washable and can be put in the dryer.

A friend of mine had given me a very cherished gift: a vintage box of yarn, carefully preserved from the 1920s. Although the original owner never knitted with the yarn, she did recognize its supe- *rior quality and had stored it well. With yarn nearly ninety years old, I decided to knit a lovely Chanel-style jacket. Just like the namesake of my jacket, there is no substitute for quality.* *Make an investment in your yarn, take care when knitting with it and treat the garment well, and you will have an heirloom piece to pass on to your children and grandchildren.*

Because novelty yarns have so much character, new knitters tend to rely on them as a design crutch, rather than expanding their knitting repertoire and developing their skills. Have fun with novelty yarn. Consider using it as a trim in a sweater, or find an interesting and unusual use for it beyond the simple scarf.

CHOOSING THE RIGHT YARNS FOR THE RIGHT PERSON

[EDITH KNIT TIPS]

Zipped for Success

Slippery yarns continually unravel off the ball, so here's a solution I offer my clients. Cut off one of the bottom corners off a ziplock bag and place your ball of yarn inside; thread your yarn through the hole and seal the bag shut. This will help keep your ball of yarn neat and prevent it from knotting.

Yarns Are Seasonal Too

Just like fashion trends are seasonal, yarns come and go and are often discontinued. So keep in mind that it's important to buy all the yarn at once for a project rather than just a couple balls at a time. This will ensure that you have enough and from the same dye lot.

Knitting for Baby.

The Debbie Bliss Baby Cashmerino is an ideal choice for knitting baby garments. It's soft because of the cashmere, but the merino wool adds a little more resilience for the frequent washings that baby clothes endure and also makes it more affordable.

Knitting for Teens.

Almost without exception, teens love bulky yarns. The look of these yarns never seems to go out of fashion, and the ponchos and scarves are fun and easy projects for easily distracted teens. Rowan makes great bulky yarns, with colors that change every season to reflect the fashions.

Don't Judge a Yarn by Its Cover

So you bought yarn and, at the time, you loved it. But when you went to knit with it some months later, you wondered, "What was I thinking?" Not so uncommon; even I do this. Since you can't return the yarn, make the most of it. I'll help my clients redesign the original project to incorporate some of the yarn as a trim or an embellishment, saving the rest for something or someone else. Your change of taste might be someone else's good fortune. If you knit an entire sweater and then decide you no longer like it, you can change the look by simply adding embellishments and buttons.

No Names

When knitting for a child, never put the child's name on the garment. This is a safety precaution, as children tend to respond to their name being called, even by a stranger.

Knitting for Adults.

When you love knitting as much as I do, it's hard to pick a favorite yarn. I find myself drawn both to ribbon yarns and to yarns with a little luster or texture, particularly the hand-dyed yarns. Ribbon yarns are great for knitting the lightweight jackets I love to wear: they knit up in a large, loose gauge, and replicate the look of woven fabric in an interesting and stylish way. Yarns that have texture or character—a sheen, some variation in color—work well when making sweater sets. With the 13,000 different yarns lining the shelves of my shop, sometimes regardless of the project a client has in mind, she hears yarn "calling her name," so she ends up going home with a completely different project. The first will just have to wait.

SARAH MICHELLE GELLAR

The first time Sarah Michelle came to the shop, she walked in and walked out. She had to move her car. With that done, Sarah Michelle sat at the table, and I taught her how to knit. A very fast learner, Sarah Michelle quickly grasped both the knit and the purl stitch. After she chose a pretty blue chunky yarn,

I wrote a simple pattern for her to follow in which she could combine the two stitches—and she was off knitting her first scarf. She loved it so much that the next day she came back with her mom, and this mother-daughter team returned almost every Saturday. During the holidays when Sarah Michelle was

filming Scooby-Doo, her mom came in with a tin of cookies, a gift from her and her daughter. One evening as I was about to close the store, I received a panicked call from Sarah Michelle's agent pleading with me not to close. The agent was en route to the store to buy a gift certificate for Sarah Michelle's birthday.

I have a strong reputation as a knowledgeable knitting resource within the knitting industry— not just among my clients and with the press but also among the knitting yarn and accessory manufacturers.

Clover Needles: *For as many years as I can remember, manufacturers have been soliciting my advice on everything from color choices to needles and trends. Ever since knitting with chunky yarns became all the rage, I strongly suggested that Mr. Okada, the CEO of Clover Needles, introduce a size 17 and 19 needle to his line. He did. One afternoon the marketing director for Clover USA, Jan Carr, came to visit, and* recounted how he had been suggesting this all along, but that his counsel had fallen on deaf ears. He said, "All it took was one of your calls to make a difference. . . . I've been suggesting this for years. You sure have a lot of influence."

The Edith Coat: *Knitting as an art has been around since the dawn of time. But only in the past several years did the knitting trend emerge. I have been credited by the media and by yarn manufacturers for contributing to knitting's resurgence. As a thank you and to my surprise, Berroco Yarns created the "Edith Coat." This elegant and stylish coat was one of the highest forms of flattery.*

Hana Silk: *Hana Silk by Noro had always sold very well at my shop. A thick, hand-dyed silk easily worked up in a size 10.5 needle. Then, just as quickly as it arrived, Noro discontinued importing Hana Silk to the United States. When I asked the manufacturer why, he said that it didn't sell around the country. I explained to him that at my shop, it practically flew off the shelves. He told me that "if yarn could sell at La Knitterie Parisienne, then it's worth reintroducing." Hana Silk continues to sell very well in my shop, and throughout the United States, to this day.*

I have received many calls from my knitters abroad. I was particularly surprised one day when I received a call from Regina, an actor, dancer, and choreographer, who was invited to Saudi Arabia to teach hip-hop to the King's daughter. Regina had forgotten her knitting instructions in the States. Fortunately, I had a copy in the store and was able to save the day.

chapter four

KNITTING TECHNIQUES

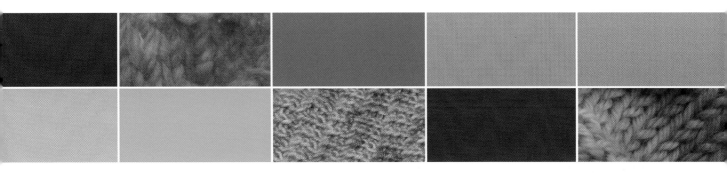

There's a simple rule to follow to determine whether your pattern will work according to the directions. Patterns may be translated improperly from another language or may just have an error. That's why it is important to read the directions before starting and also brush up on your math skills to check on the calculations as you increase and decrease.

As your knitting skills progress, you should begin to think about knitting your first, more challenging project—possibly your first sweater. The first step in making a well-fitting sweater is to take the time to take proper measurements so you can be assured that the finished garment will fit you based on the measurements and the schematics provided in the instructions.

One of the most important modern advances in knitting patterns has been the introduction of schematics: the outline drawings that indicate the final measurements of a garment. To use this to your best advantage, you will need the precise measurements of your own figure (or that of the person for whom you are knitting). Take time to obtain accurate measurements. Not only will this allow you to choose the correct size in a commercial pattern, but it is also the first step to learning how to design your own sweaters.

TAKING YOUR MEASUREMENTS

Take your measurements and mark them down, updating them from time to time. Understanding what they mean, and how you can use them to adapt existing patterns or write your own, is a crucial step to becoming an accomplished knitter. Note that these are "actual measurements" and don't account for how your garment will actually fit you. The standard allowance for a sweater's normal fitting is about 10 percent more. For a looser-fitting garment, allow about 15 percent more.

- Bust/Chest Size: Hold a measuring tape around your bust, measuring the circumference starting from the left underarm. Hold the edges of the tape measure to the side, under your arm, and not the front; this will provide a more accurate measurement. Measurements taken from the front can result in the bust/chest size being as much as 2 inches off.

- Back: Hold the tape measure from shoulder blade to shoulder blade.

- Neck: Measure across the back of the neck.

- Arm Length: With your arm down at your side, measure from 1 inch below the armpit to your wrist.

- Upper Arm: Measure the fullest part of your arm.

- Wrist, Waist, Hip: Place the tape measure around these body parts.

- Desired Length of Sweater: With your arm at your side, measure from one inch below the armpit to your desired length.

[EDITH KNIT TIP]

Learning to Read a Pattern

Always read your pattern first. Circle the number pertinent to your size. Make sure that you understand what the symbols in the knitting pattern mean, for instance, commas, parentheses, a repeat. Then start knitting!

The great thing about knitting is that no matter what your size, you can customize a pattern to meet your specifications. As a shop owner, I meet and design for all types of women, in all shapes and sizes. What might look adorable on a smaller, petite frame won't necessarily work on a broader, full-figure woman. That's when I have to assert a certain level of discretion and diplomacy. I help many women to make more appropriate designs to flatter their figures.

USING YOUR MEASUREMENTS TO ADAPT PATTERNS

People come in all shapes and sizes, and so do arm lengths, so it's important not to skip this step and to realize that the lengths of the sleeves may vary. Nothing looks worse than a sleeve that is either too long or too short.

Before you attempt to modify your sleeves, you must understand two important facts of sleeve construction. First, sleeves generally look best when all the increases are spaced out over the first 12 inches of the sleeve. Second, you should have 5 inches of straight knitting between the last increase and the point where you first cast off to shape the armhole. When altering the measurements of a sleeve, it's important to maintain these proportions in order to have a well-fitting sleeve.

You can modify the length of a sleeve as follows:

- When shortening the sleeve by 3 inches, you will do all your increases over the first 9 inches rather than 12. Remember, you want to knit your last increase 5 inches before your armhole shaping begins.

- When shortening your sleeves by 2 inches, with a new total length of 15 inches before armhole shaping, you want to knit your last increase at 10 inches. To determine how to space out your increases, first figure out your row gauge. For example, if your row gauge is 6 rows per inch, you will have 2 inches of ribbing and 13 inches of stockinette before you begin shaping your armhole. You will calculate your increase as follows: 6 rows per inch times 13 inches of stockinette means that you have 78 rows to space your increases. According to your pattern, you have to increase 8 stitches on each side. To do this, divide 8 into 78. You need to increase every 9.75 rows. Since you obviously can't split a row in half, you will need to increase every 9th and every 10th row alternately, 8 times.

ALTERING A BUST MEASUREMENT

When selecting your desired size, you'll need to account for ease in the fit of your sweater. For instance, if you have a 36-inch chest and want a form-fitting sweater, you should still allow for an inch of ease on each piece and knit a size 38-inch sweater. If the pattern doesn't allow for your size, you can use your measurements to help figure out a size that will fit you. For example, if you are a 40-inch chest, you'll need to make a garment that is a size 42. However, if on the pattern you find that the biggest size listed is only a 40, you will need to do some recalculating. Adjusting the pattern so that it will be your size is easy if you follow these basic steps:

- First note the stitch gauge of the sweater. You will need this information to recalculate the number of stitches to cast on for your work.

- Since the sweater is a size 40, both the front and the back should each measure 20 inches. You need to add 1 inch of ease to both the front and the back. If you are a size 42, multiply 21 by the gauge of the sweater. That will give you the number of stitches that you need to cast on. If you want it the same length, you will keep the increases the same; when you get to the armholes, you will have to calculate the depth of the armhole you need. You will basically have to recreate the measurements for this.

- To calculate the amount of stitches needed to form an armhole, you'll need to leave enough stitches for the shoulder and the neck, calculated as follows and taking into account the measurements of both the shoulders and the neck. For instance, if your shoulder measures 3.5 inches and your neck 7 inches, you'll need to leave 14 inches of stitches. If your gauge is 5 stitches

Years ago, sweaters were knitted very form-fitting, so to compensate for the bust, the front was knitted larger than the back. This style is out of fashion now

and rarely done. Should you want to knit a sweater in this fashion, however, you will have to calculate the front and the back measurements separately,

and apply the same formula to each to figure out the new number of stitches to cast on.

to 1 inch, the amount will be 70 stitches. If you need 21 inches for a sweater, times 5 to 1 inch, or 105 stitches, you'll need to subtract 35 stitches from the total amount, or round it up to 36 stitches as you will need an even amount for both armholes, therefore shaping your armhole by decreasing 18 stitches on each side.

SHAPING A NECKLINE

Certain measurements are standard. The back of a woman's neck is nearly always 6.5 or 7 inches. Assuming your neck is 7 inches, you will need to put 36 stitches on a stitch holder for the back neck. To shape the front neck, you'll need to put half that number of stitches in the center of the sweater—in this case, 18 stitches—on a stitch holder and decrease 9 stitches on each side. You will now have the same number of stitches bound off at the front as you have across the back neck.

Unlike with fabric where you can simply cut the material to form the curve that shapes the neckline, with knitting you must form a curve by putting stitches on a holder and progressively binding off and decreasing to form a slight curve. When making a crew neck, I suggest putting the center stitches on a holder instead of binding them off. This will make it easier to find those stitches when you are ready to pick them up to make the border rather than guessing which stitches to pick up. This will also create a stronger and neater edge. The same applies when making a cardigan. I suggest putting the first inch of stitches on a holder. Therefore my pattern will read as follows: knit or purl 5 stitches, put them on a holder, then every other row bind off 2 stitches 1 time, knit 2 stitches together 3 times, thus forming a gentle curve.

PICKING UP STITCHES FOR A CREW NECK OR ROUND NECK

Always use a circular needle no longer than 16 inches when knitting a neck. Starting at the back at the right shoulder, pick up and knit the first and all remaining stitches from the holder. Continue as follows: Insert the tip of your needle under the 2 bars of the edge of your sweater, wrap the yarn around it counterclockwise, draw that loop onto your right-hand needle, go to the 2 bars immediately following, and repeat this process. You will be picking up 3 stitches in a row immediately next to each other, then skipping a space. If you fail to do so and pick up every stitch, your border will be too wide and will ruffle. If you skip too many spaces, your neck will be too tight and you might not be able to put your head through the neck opening. When picking up the neck of a cardigan, place the sweater with the front facing you. Starting with the stitches on the holder for the left front, pick up and knit the first and remaining stitches on the holder, and continue picking up 3 stitches in a row and skipping 1 for the curve of the neck. Then pick up all the stitches on the holder for the back of the neck and repeat this process of picking up 3 stitches in a row and skipping 1 until you reach the last stitch on the holder of the right front. Picking up 3 stitches in a row and skipping 1 is commonly referred to as the "Rule of 3."

PICKING UP A BORDER

Unfortunately we cannot leave stitches on a holder when picking up a horizontal border, but the same "Rule of 3" applies. Insert the point of the needle under the 2 bars formed by the end of your knitting. Wrap your yarn around it counterclockwise, gently pull it through the front of your work, and place it on your right-hand needle. The stitch is made. Continue across the row until the desired number of stitches have been picked up.

MAKING BUTTONHOLES

To make a buttonhole, the rule to follow is that the buttonholes for a man's cardigan are on the left side and on the right side for a woman's. You'll have to apply mathematical skill when creating buttonholes. Buttonholes are usually made starting 3 stitches from the bottom edge and finishing 3 stitches from the top, with the rest of the buttonholes spaced evenly across the border. Let's say, for instance, that you need 5

INSERT THE TIP OF YOUR NEEDLE UNDER THE 2 BARS OF THE EDGE OF YOUR SWEATER

PULL YARN THROUGH LOOP AND KNIT THAT STITCH

PICK A SECOND LOOP

KNIT THAT LOOP

CONTINUE TO PICK 3 STITCHES IN A ROW—SKIP ONE

buttonholes, each made of 2 spaces, and your border is composed of 92 stitches. Your calculations should be as follows: 3 stitches from the bottom, 3 stitches from the top, 5 openings of 2 stitches. You will need to deduct 16 stitches from the total of 92 stitches, leaving 76 stitches. For 5 buttons, you'll need 4 spaces. Divide 4 into 76 and that will tell you that you need to knit 19 stitches between your buttonholes.

To make a buttonhole of 2 or more stitches:

STEP 1: Leaving the yarn untouched on the right-hand side, slip the first 2 stitches of the left-hand needle purlwise.

STEP 2: With your left-hand needle, lift the first stitch over the second and slip it over, then repeat this process one more time.

STEP 3: Place the remaining stitch back on the left-hand needle. Turn your work.

STEP 4: Placing your right-hand needle between that stitch and the next stitch on the left-hand needle, draw a loop, twist it, and place it on the right-hand needle. You now have replaced the first bound stitch of your buttonhole. Repeat this process until all your stitches have been replaced.

STEP 5: Turn your work and continue knitting or ribbing until your next buttonhole has to be made.

STEP 1A

STEP 1B

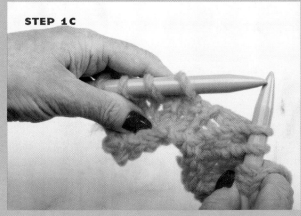

STEP 1C

STEP 2A

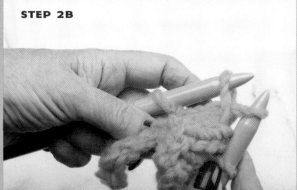

STEP 2B

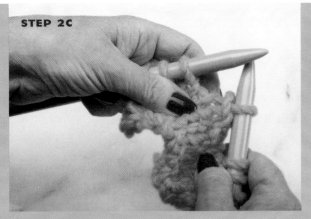

STEP 2C

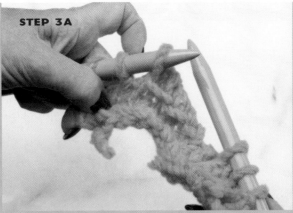

STEP 3A

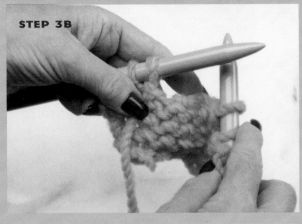

STEP 3B

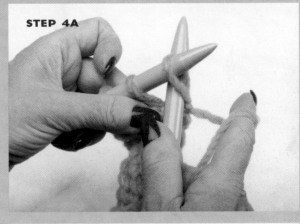

STEP 4A

STEP 4B

STEP 4C

STEP 5A

STEP 5B

Adding Length or Shortening a Finished Sweater

After you've completed your sweater, you realize your garment has turned out either too long or too short. If it's too short, determine whether it can be blocked to the correct size. If this doesn't work, you can still salvage it with a seemingly dramatic but really quite simple technique.

You've sewn your sweater together, blocked it, and it is still two inches too short. Here's what you need to do. Take a knitting needle and insert it into a stitch a couple of rows above the ribbing. Gently pull at the stitch to create a loop and then cut the loop in half. Gently tug at the top and bottom of the sweater, which will separate neatly along the "pull line." Use a smaller-size knitting needle than the one used to knit the garment, pick up the stitches on the main body, transfer to the original-size needle, and start knitting. Though it may seem odd, knitting doesn't have an up or down direction. Even though you are now knitting in the opposite direction, your new stitches won't look any different from your original ones. Knit until the body of the sweater is your desired length, then change your needle size, work your ribbing, and cast off.

If your sweater is too long, you'll follow the same process, taking into account that you will need to add the ribbing so you will need to shorten accordingly.

STEP 1

STEP 4

STEP 7

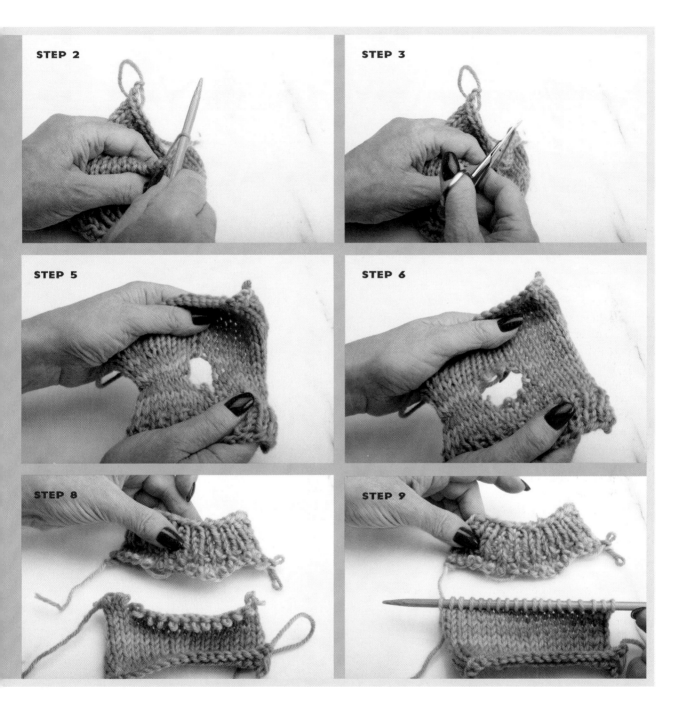

STEP 2

STEP 3

STEP 5

STEP 6

STEP 8

STEP 9

Knowing how to reknit sections of your sweater, as I just described to you, is an invaluable skill. Recently, a client of mine, Laura, went on a family weekend to a log cabin in a state park. Bliss! She took her knitting, parked herself by the lake, and worked on a beautiful angora sweater for her daughter. That night an animal sneaked into the cabin and dined on the sweater, leaving a huge hole in the sleeve. When she showed up at my shop on Tuesday she was hysterical. Her hard work was wasted and her daughter was disappointed. They don't call me the guru for nothing! I showed her how to separate the sleeve as shown on the previous page, then pick up her stitches and reknit the sleeve. Crisis averted.

[EDITH **KNIT TIPS**]

Buttonholes for Men and Women

Here's a simple phrase to remind you which side the buttonholes go on for a man's garment vs. a woman's: "Buttonhole on right side as women are always right!"

If you are making a vertical border on a cardigan, I suggest that after you have finished the bottom border for the front, you leave the first inch on a holder then continue in pattern for the rest of the sweater. When you are ready to make the border, place the stitches that are left on hold for that border back on your needles and proceed in the stitch of your choice. When making a vertical buttonhole, split your work in half, attach another ball of yarn, and work the two sides separately for the desired length of the buttonhole, then cut one of the balls of yarn and join the two pieces back together. Repeat this process for the desired number of buttonholes. When the border is finished, simply sew it to the body of the sweater.

MAKING THE BORDER OF A V-NECK

For V-neck borders, you will need a 24-inch circular needle. When designing a V-neck sweater, you will need an odd number of stitches in order to divide your work equally. Put the center stitch on a plastic safety pin when shaping the neck, placing a stitch marker on either side of that center stitch. To make the border, start at the right back shoulder; pick up and knit your stitches in the same manner as for the crew neck. When ribbing your border, the stitch in the center will always be worked as a knit stitch, and it is on either side of that stitch that you will decrease by either knitting or purling two stitches together to form a mitered edge, the slant that forms the neck shaping.

chapter five

PERFECT FINISHING

I love to see my knitters discover their abilities and explore their imaginations. There is nothing more satisfying than seeing a knitter find the art in their craft.

As important as it is to master the basics of knitting—knit, purl, make one—none of your hard work will add up to anything if you don't understand how to finish your knitting correctly. In this chapter, I'll show you how to sew the pieces of your sweater together, block, or shape, the final garment.

There is a reason why finishers charge a lot of money to put a sweater together. Anyone can knit the pieces of a sweater, but not everyone has the eye for detail or the patience needed to finish it well. Finishing can take a lot of time, so be aware that it may take as long to finish your sweater as it took to knit it. Don't try to rush this last but equally important process. Instead, take as much pride and pleasure in finishing your garment as you did in knitting it.

SEAMING

Once you have finished knitting the pieces of your sweater, your final steps will be to seam them together and block the finished garment. Don't rush either of these steps. Quality seaming will take you a while, but it's critical if you are going to achieve a smooth and refined end result.

As with every technique in knitting, there are various ways to sew a sweater together, but I teach several specific skills to my knitters that cover just about any seaming situation. To seam the main pieces of the sweater, I generally recommend "weaving," which is also referred to as the mattress stitch. I prefer to weave, but it's not always possible. I recently made a suit out of a fine yarn that I found very difficult to weave together because the yarn was uneven. So I used another method, "backstitching." To put the shoulders together, I used the three-needle bind-off and omitted the process of staggered cast-offs that most patterns call for.

Weaving. Weaving, or the mattress stitch, is the most common seaming technique and resembles the zigzag of shoe lacing. It's easy, invisible to the eye, and leaves a neat seam on the inside. To weave you need to place the front piece and the back piece side by side, with the right side facing up. One side will almost certainly be shorter or tighter than the other, so don't be afraid to pull and adjust it if necessary.

As you weave the sides, you will notice that there are evenly spaced bumps on every other row. The goal is to have every bump fit neatly into the space opposite it. You'll apply the shoe-lacing motion, interlocking

[EDITH **KNIT TIP**]

To Block— Before or After?

There is a certain amount of debate in the knitting world about whether to block your sweater before or after you sew it together. I view blocking a garment as an opportunity to refine the fit and shape of your sweater–something you can only do when the sweater is seamed and you are able to try it on.

one piece to the other. When you've worked a few rows, pull your seaming thread taut; the knitting should neatly align, leaving an almost invisible seam on the wrong side.

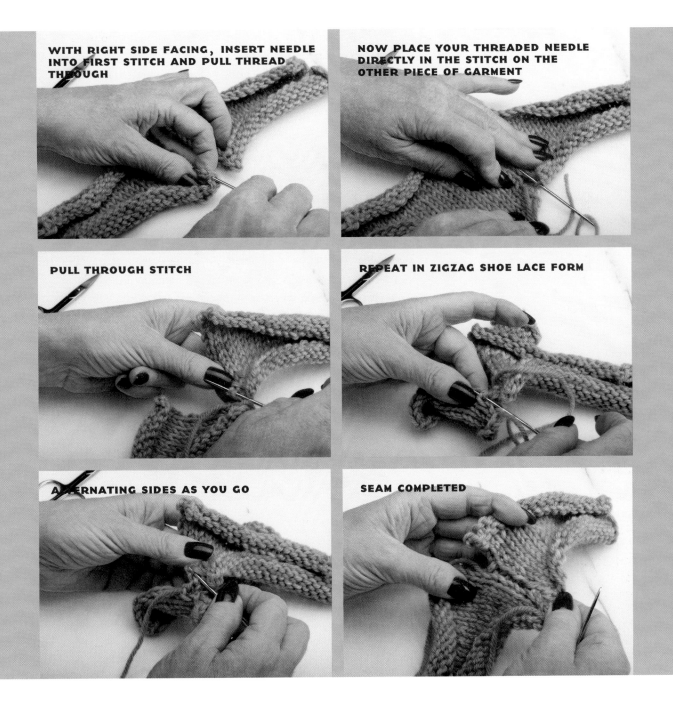

WITH RIGHT SIDE FACING, INSERT NEEDLE INTO FIRST STITCH AND PULL THREAD THROUGH

NOW PLACE YOUR THREADED NEEDLE DIRECTLY IN THE STITCH ON THE OTHER PIECE OF GARMENT

PULL THROUGH STITCH

REPEAT IN ZIGZAG SHOE LACE FORM

ALTERNATING SIDES AS YOU GO

SEAM COMPLETED

Knit and Sew with Different Yarns

Don't sew your sweater together with the yarn you used to knit it. Every so often, a knitter will come in with a beautiful sweater that he or she has painstakingly sewn together—incorrectly. When I help take it apart, I make a terrible discovery: despite my advice, the knitter has chosen to sew the sweater together with the same yarn used to knit it. I can't stress this point enough: don't do this. Using the same yarn to seam as you did to knit only leads to tears, because it can be almost impossible to see your stitches to undo them, plus you run the risk of cutting your hard labored work. Instead, I recommend using a tapestry wool in a matching shade to sew your garment together. When sewing your cotton, rayon, or silk sweater together, use either embroidery floss or pearl cotton.

Backstitch.

Backstitching is similar to the stitch made by a sewing machine and is very firm because you work over the seam twice. If you've ever hand-sewn a seam, you will be familiar with this technique. Backstitching is the simple motion of stitching forward one stitch, then bringing your needle back to reenter the fabric halfway down that stitch. So basically for every stitch worked, you are only moving forward half a stitch.

- Put the two pieces you will be sewing on top of each other, with the right sides facing inward (as if the finished sweater has been turned inside out and is lying flat). Take a few moments to make sure the edges of the sweater where you will be seaming are fully aligned. Using straight pins, pin the edges together as close to the edge as possible.

- Thread embroidery floss or yarn through a darning needle that is similar in color to your knitting yarn, and insert the needle through both layers of knitting at the bottom of the sweater. Backstitch several times to secure your thread. Now work up the sides, always backstitching as you go.

THREE-NEEDLE BIND-OFF

Although most patterns suggest binding off the shoulders and then sewing them together, I prefer the three-needle bind-off method because it results in a smooth, clean, and invisible shoulder seam. It's also much easier to do. There is nothing more unsightly than a bulky shoulder seam. Remember to take into account that you must knit the stitches for the shoulder that would have otherwise been cast off.

When you've finished the back and front of your sweater, don't bind off the shoulders. Instead, place those stitches on a stitch holder, leaving a long tail of yarn about four times the length of your shoulder to knit the shoulders together, then cut the yarn. With the right sides of the sweater facing each other, replace the stitch holders with your knitting needles,

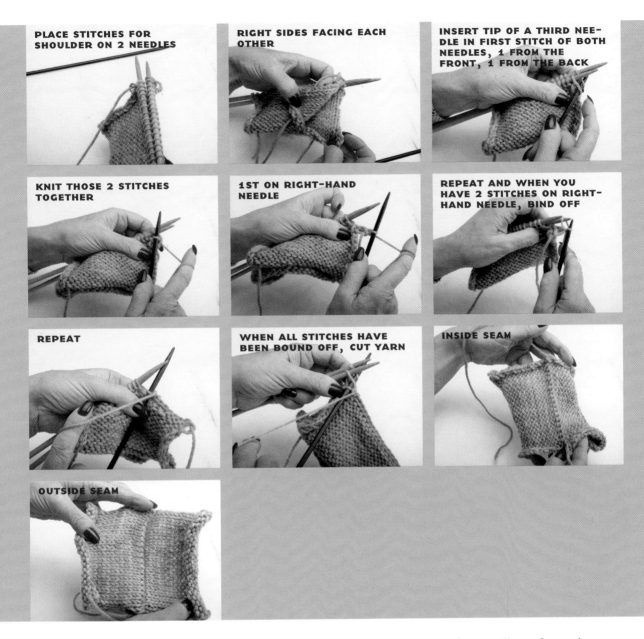

PLACE STITCHES FOR SHOULDER ON 2 NEEDLES

RIGHT SIDES FACING EACH OTHER

INSERT TIP OF A THIRD NEEDLE IN FIRST STITCH OF BOTH NEEDLES, 1 FROM THE FRONT, 1 FROM THE BACK

KNIT THOSE 2 STITCHES TOGETHER

1ST ON RIGHT-HAND NEEDLE

REPEAT AND WHEN YOU HAVE 2 STITCHES ON RIGHT-HAND NEEDLE, BIND OFF

REPEAT

WHEN ALL STITCHES HAVE BEEN BOUND OFF, CUT YARN

INSIDE SEAM

OUTSIDE SEAM

taking care to make sure the two points of the needle are facing the same direction. Take a third needle to join the shoulders together. Insert the third needle into the first stitch of the other two needles and knit them together. Next, knit the second two stitches together. When you have two stitches on your right-hand needle, bind them off. Repeat across the row, binding off as you go. Note that the needles replacing the stitch holders function as holders themselves, so you can use a different size needle as long as your third needle is the same size you used to knit your sweater.

Stitch Holders

When using stitch holders, it's a good idea to turn them upside down on your work so that should it open up accidentally, your stitches won't fall off.

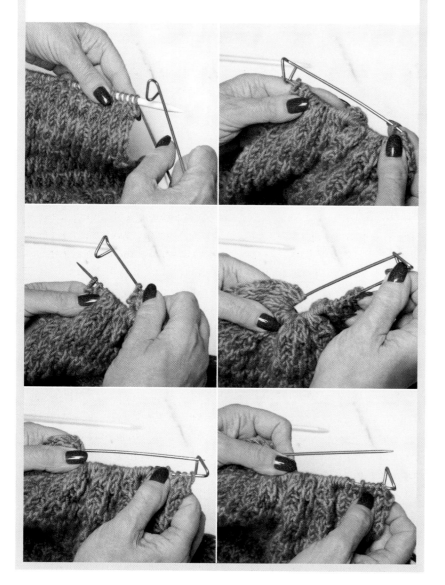

Ah, success! You've successfully completed your very first sweater. Congratulations. Everyone's quite impressed with your work. Only you seem to notice that it needs some minor adjustments: it could have been a bit roomier in the body, or perhaps you want the seams pressed. There is a simple solution. It's called blocking.

BLOCKING

Blocking is the process by which you dampen your finished garment with cold water and, pinning it onto a towel, gently stretch it until it dries in the shape that the pattern called for.

Find a large flat area to lay out your towel and garment where it can remain undisturbed for at least a day. If it's exposed to sunshine, so much the better—it will help to dry your sweater even faster—but avoid direct light as it might fade the color. Special blocking boards are also available for purchase, but this is not essential. What is essential is stainless steel T-shaped blocking pins. These are heavier than ordinary straight pins you might use in sewing, and they won't rust.

Here are few tips to help you learn to block:

• I recommend you use the schematic from your pattern as a guide. Or, if you prefer, you can take one of your favorite sweaters that is similar in shape as a guide to block your gar-

Remember Where You Put It . . .

When you are seaming your sweater, you need to bury the loose end of your seaming thread. However, keep in mind there may be a time when you might need to undo the seaming, so you'll want to make sure you leave a bit of the tail visible.

ment. Lay the damp sweater on the towel and pin out the shoulders, starting from the center. Make sure your pins don't push through the actual material, but rather just through the yarn loops at the edge of the sweater, and take care to use enough pins to ensure that your yarn won't stretch unevenly.

- If you want to make your sweater a little wider or longer, gently pull the sweater either outward or downward as you pin along the top, sides, and bottom. While you are pulling it into shape, remember to *ease* the sweater, rather than tugging on it roughly. Refer back to your schematic or guide sweater as you go.

Once you've finished blocking your garment, check to ensure that the edges of your sweater have smooth lines. Now leave it to dry.

Another technique for shaping a finished garment is steaming, an even easier process than blocking. Start by laying a dry towel on an ironing board or a flat surface, then place your garment on the towel. Next, take a very wet (but not dripping) towel and lay it on your knitting. Using a warm setting on your iron, lightly steam over the towel, quickly and gently touching it. Leave the wet towel in place on the garment overnight. The weight of the towel will be enough to block your garment. In the morning, remove the towel and let it air-dry.

CLEANING YOUR GARMENT

Fill up a plastic tub with cold water and add a capful of Eucalan—an Australian product made from the eucalyptus plant, which I happen to find to be one of the most effective, safest, and most gentle cleansers. I only recommend this, as some popular wool wash detergents will discolor your yarn. The choice of washing agent is more important than you may realize. Washing dyed natural yarns may fade the color, and washing garments made of animal fibers, such as wool or cashmere, causes them to lose their lanolin—the natural oil in animal fiber that keeps the garment soft and protects the individual fibers from breakage. Once you have washed a sweater several times, you have effectively stripped it of its lanolin, and your sweater will lose its elasticity and softness. Eucalan and other similar washing agents on the market restore the vibrancy and life of the fabric. Trust me, you'll be amazed.

Washing Wisely

To avoid the risk of felting your garment, only use cold water and let it soak for the recommend time noted on the label. When using Eucalan or like products, do not rinse; just gently squeeze (and don't ring it) out the excess water. Preferably, place the garment in the spin cycle of your washing machine to remove the excess water. Lay it on a flat surface to dry.

FIXING MINOR MISTAKES

At some point, every knitter is bound to make a mistake—sometimes it's small and other times it's colossal. Perhaps there's a purl when you should have knitted, or your cable twisted in the wrong direction. The result is devastating and you see it as a glaring mistake. These are heartwrenching moments. For some mysterious reason, such mistakes tend to be in the most obvious place. What to do? Well, the first thing to do is put the piece down and walk away, thus avoiding your first impulse to rip it out or toss it. After you've had a chance to compose yourself, you can begin to think about how to fix it.

There are several ways to fix a mistake or remedy a problem, other than ripping out your entire work. One of the first thing you can do is put away the pattern and look at your creation objectively. So your sweater looks a bit different than the original design. Let's make the best of the worst. I've had women come in with sweaters that had been ruined by bleach spots—we embroidered over them or added a decorative item. Sweaters that were too small—we added a side panel to both sides to increase the circumference. Be brave and make a design feature out of your mistake. The key is to not be afraid to take risks in repairing your work.

Remember that your knitting is a flexible, forgiving medium. If you can approach your problem creatively, you can probably figure out a way to work with it. Here are some knitting mistakes we've encountered at the store and the solutions we found to fix them.

• One of my clients, Jodi, is very creative and passionate about her knitting. She only makes a few pieces a year and strives to make them perfect and beautiful. Unfortunately, they don't always end up as perfect as they could, since she doesn't always heed my advice. This January her big project was a pretty, hot pink cardigan, knitted in a bulky wool, with a long fringe trim around the edges. The sweater turned out lopsided, with one side of the front hanging lower than the other. Disaster. Jodi was distraught. I looked at it for a minute and realized that all we had to do was a little nip 'n' tuck. Instead of ripping out the front, I threaded a piece of yarn up the sagging side, hiding the thread between the heavy fringe and the front band. As the other women in the knitting circle looked on, I pulled gently at the yarn until the fronts were even and then anchored the yarn at the neckline, making sure the stitches were evenly spaced along the band. This isn't always the solution for sagging sweaters, especially if they sag more than one inch, but it worked with her design.

- Eliza is a sporadic knitter. I may see her every day for a month, then not see her for a year. Because she doesn't knit consistently, her work often has flaws. Recently she came in with a poncho she had just completed. The neck was far too wide and slid annoyingly down her shoulders. I knew that if Eliza couldn't save this project, she'd probably give up knitting for good, so I devised a way to fix it. I suggested she crochet a band around the neck, working with a contrasting yarn so it looked like a design feature. However, instead of picking up every stitch, I had her pick up three stitches for every four, ending up with forty-five stitches instead of the sixty she started with. This narrowed the neckline enough so that the poncho now sat comfortably on her shoulders. Eliza was happy with the result, and she even comes to the knitting circle a little more frequently than she did before.

- Felting is a one-way process; it can't be undone—most of the time. A newcomer to the shop's knitting circle had spent many months finishing a mohair sweater—only to find that her very efficient housekeeper had ruined it in the washer and dryer. I didn't want her to become discouraged and throw in the knitting towel. I wasn't sure whether I could fix this felting problem, but I intended to try a process that had worked for me in the past. I took her sweater home and immersed it in cold water in my washing machine, using a highly sudsy shampoo, like Prell. I let it soak overnight, then ran the spin

TO ERR IS HUMAN

Take a look at a sweater you purchased from a department store. No matter what the style, you know the tension will be perfect, the stitch work flawless. Machines don't make mistakes. If you find a flaw in your hand-knit sweater, don't be disheartened by it. That flaw means you're human, and it reflects the uniqueness of your work, proof that, unlike mass-produced sweaters, yours is one of a kind. For example, did you know that when you tour the United Nations, the guide will point out the flaws in the most amazing handmade wall hangings, explaining, "If it was perfect, it would have been made by the hands of God." In fact, I have a client who purposely leaves one wrong stitch in her work. This stems from the time she accidentally made a slight mistake and refused to rip it out. This has become her trademark.

Joining in the Round with a Circular Needle

Joining in the round is the process by which you join the beginning and the end of a row together to create a continuous circle. Joining in the round can be tricky. I suggest to first knit or purl a row, then join as this will prevent the row from twisting.

cycle *without rinsing it,* and stretched it into shape and let it dry. The delicate mohair blossomed again, and the sweater was almost as good as new. When I gave it to her, I suggested she "not wear this one in the rain."

- Rather than toss that oversized sweater from the '80s, you might consider cutting it down to size. You'll want to find a tailor who has a serger machine to prevent the stitches from running as the sweater is cut and sewn back together.

- One of my clients ran out of wool for her scarf and I didn't have any more, so I divided a ball of novelty yarn, and we knitted at either end of the scarf so that the different yarn was a design feature rather than a fix.

The point of these stories is to encourage you to look creatively at your mistakes, and to devise your own solutions by approaching your errors rationally and analytically. Check your emotions at the door, until you've devised a solution.

TAL MEIRSON

A high-profile production supervisor, Tal's résumé includes such hits as the Academy Award–winning film Million Dollar Baby, *starring Hilary Swank and Clint Eastwood;* The Human Stain, *starring Nicole Kidman and Anthony Hopkins; and* The Mothman Prophecies, *starring Debra Messing and Richard Gere. Tal is a high-powered Hollywood executive whose position comes with a certain level of stress. Tal*

walked into my shop one afternoon to learn to knit. She'd heard that knitting was relaxing and therapeutic and needed to take the steam out of her pressure-cooker life. Ironically, the biggest stress in her life was caused by her fear of flying. After a recent trip back to Los Angeles from Tokyo, Tal came to show me her scarf. It had to be at least thirteen feet long and was riddled with dropped stitches. "I know this isn't my

best work," she said sarcastically, "but I think I owe my sanity to this scarf. My seventeen-hour flight was filled with eleven hours of turbulence, and I thought I was going to die. Then I started to knit. It was the only thing that kept me from having a total panic attack. To tell you the truth, with every stitch, I literally felt the stress ebbing from my body."

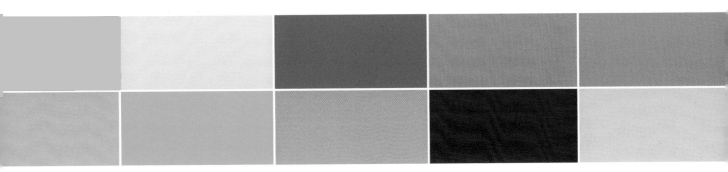

EMOTIONAL KNITTING

Besides the obvious pleasure of owning a successful business, one thing I find truly gratifying about La Knitterie Parisienne is that it enables me to help my knitters reconnect with something important that is missing in their lives, to feel some connection to their mothers and grandmothers, to their roots. When I first came to America, knitting was a solitary activity; I was the first to reintroduce the idea of social knitting to a new generation.

For me, the knitting experience has always been a social one; in my first store, The Canvas Pad, I encouraged people to sit and linger and work on their projects. What was popular in New Jersey has exploded into a cultural phenomenon in Los Angeles; whether it's Wednesday nights or Friday mornings, I always have people sitting at my table, chatting, knitting, and enjoying each other's company.

I love this aspect of what I do. In a city like Los Angeles, where everyone is from somewhere else, it's hard to meet people and develop friendships, and even harder to replace that feeling of having older female relatives—a mother you can call on when you feel out of your depth. Always available at my fingertips is a long phone list of my regular customers—they are more than clients, they are friends. We have dinner, share the holidays, and know and care about each other's good and bad times. Just because a pregnant member of the knitting circle is confined to bed rest does not mean she is out of the loop: I will call her from the hubbub of Wednesday night so she can talk to her friends and feel part of the circle again.

SEEN & HEARD AT LA KNITTERIE PARISIENNE, PART 1

Edith's ability to understand your work is amazing. You can know something is wrong but not know what it is. So you hold up your work from across the room and she will say, "Third row down, about halfway across—rip!" She's seen the mistake, and she already knows what you have to do.

I've been coming to La Knitterie Parisienne for years now, and all my family know that it's really helped to keep me grounded, give me somewhere to go to be with friends and just relax. A few months ago my mom called me on my cell phone with some bad news—the first thing she said was "Yoli, are you knitting," and I said "No," and she said, "I wish you were . . ."

I guess I've spent too much of my life here, because every so often my husband will call me and say, "Honey, I'm driving past the store now, shall I throw some food and water through the door?"

My husband was so excited when I started knitting, because he thought he'd save money since I was shopping at a yarn store instead of the Beverly Center. When I finally brought him in, he looked at a beautiful Prism scarf and said, "That's gorgeous," and Edith said, "Of course it is, that's a $95 scarf," and my poor husband replied, "Do you have anything else?"

Drive to Edith's shop: 1 hour. Cost of gas: $6. Sitting at Edith's table: priceless.

It's so wonderful. I knit two rows here, two rows there. I can relax for ten minutes.

It's added to my life; it's more than a knit shop.

"You're too stressed, go knit at La Knitterie Parisienne for a couple of hours," said one husband to his wife!

The best words Edith can ever say to you are "Bring it here, I'll fix it."

This sense of community is what I mean by "emotional knitting," and it's what I hope in this chapter to help you to create for yourself. Over the years I've been called upon to organize customized knitting socials for countless celebrities. The baby-blanket social is always the most popular, but there are dozens of other holidays and special events that can be organized around a knitting party—the only limit is your imagination.

ORGANIZING YOUR KNITTING SOCIAL

There are two kinds of knitting socials. The first is organized to accomplish a specific task, for instance, to make a baby blanket for an expectant mother. The second kind is organized for purely social reasons, perhaps to try and jump start a knitting group at your local coffee shop. In either situation, you need to consider the same basics: location, materials, guests, and theme. As knitting socials become more popular, you'll need to be adventurous to draw guests.

"I couldn't stop, didn't have time to stop, but my car stopped anyway."
  Debra Messing

"You made me an addict."
  Caroline Rhea, on opening the door to my shop on her way to dinner.

"I program my car. It only knows one way . . . to your store."
  Susan Tolsky

In all my years in business, it was Carnie Wilson who pointed out something I'd never noticed before about the store.

"Edith," she said, "did you notice there isn't a clock anywhere to be found? Your store is like a casino. The hours fly by and I don't even realize it."

One client who was in the shop with some time to spare suddenly got up shrieking, "Oh my gosh, I forgot my doctor's appointment!"

The first thing you'll want to do is find a location. Coffee shops are good, if a little predictable—make sure the owner is comfortable with her tables and chairs being taken over. Keep your eyes open for more interesting venues, like the London-based knitters who hold their knitting group on the Circle line of the Underground, or hold socials at friends' homes on a rotating basis.

Keep it easy and simple. Knitting parties are most enjoyable when the hostess has created an ingenious theme for the party. You'll also want to be sure to have enough experienced knitters on hand to encourage and lead beginners.

- Decide on a budget. Are your guests going to contribute? If you have ten or more guests I would estimate about $15 for materials per person, and don't forget to include additional costs for food and beverages. Depending on the yarn you select, you can expect to pay about $7 to $10 a ball. Splurge a little for needles. Clover bamboo needles are a great choice; they are nonslippery, light, and easy for beginners to use. They also feel good in your hands, which may encourage your new knitters to keep knitting after your party.

CAMRYN MANHEIM'S BABY SHOWER

I had received a call from my friend and client Caroline Rhea asking for help organizing a baby shower for Camryn Manheim. "Do you have any ideas?" she asked me. That's when I conceived the idea of hosting a "baby-blanket knitting party," where each guest would knit a square for the blanket. The now famous baby shower knitting party was born. It's rewarding to know that my orig-inal idea started a national trend. I knew that many of the invited actresses were knitters already, but to get the fun going without any hiccups I precast dozens of needles with luxurious yarns in a cheerful color palette—yellow, white, and green. As the dozens of guests— sixty-four to be exact, including Lara Flynn Boyle, Brooke Shields, Calista Flockhart, and Marlee Matlin, to name a few— took their places, my daughters, Natalie and Audrey, and I hopped from table to table, teaching, picking up dropped stitches, encouraging the beginners, and casting off when necessary. The party was a huge success. It was the very first baby-blanket knitting party of its kind, and pictures from it were featured in all the celebrity magazines.

I happened to be watching The Caroline Rhea Show *one day when Jane Krakowski was a guest. During the show, they started to banter about knitting, and Caroline mentioned my name. Caroline had thrown Camryn Manheim's baby shower, and I had taught Jane, who was a guest at the baby shower, how to knit. Since they both knew me, I suddenly became the subject, and then Jane—who is also originally from Parsippany, New Jersey— announced that her mother and I had known each other for years!*

HOSTING YOUR BABY-BLANKET PARTY

It's easy to throw your own baby-blanket knitting party. You don't even need to be an expert knitter; just follow my guidelines.

- You'll need 36 six-by-six-inch squares for a blanket. To ensure your guests finish their squares at the party, go for a relatively big gauge; 3 or 4 stitches to an inch. If you end up with more squares than you need, make another blanket: that's what we did for Camryn Manheim. This also happens to be the *only* time it's not necessary for each guest to make a gauge—originality is relished.

- Buy good-quality yarn. There's no point in having twenty friends work together for an afternoon if the result is a scratchy mess of acrylic. I recommend buying a heavy cotton yarn, like Pronto or Goa, knitted on size 10 or 10.5 needles so the results can be achieved quickly.

- Set up your tables, or, if you prefer, cluster your couch and armchairs together for an informal, cozy feel. Arrange the yarns and needles in small containers, one per guest. For Camryn's shower we used wicker baskets, but you might use giant coffee cups or cute shopping bags from your local yarn store, whatever seems to fit your theme the best. Have a few good reference books on hand for the more adventurous knitters, though most people will inevitably knit garter-stitch squares, and mistakes only add to the charm of the blanket.

- As the host, if you're not proficient in finishing the blanket, bring it to your local yarn store and they can advise you.

After learning to knit at Camryn Manheim's baby shower, Brooke | *enjoyed it so much that she would frequent my shop, which is located around the corner* | *from her gym, and sit and chat with her fellow knitters.*

KIDS KNIT

There was a reason why knitting was an integral part of my childhood education in Paris. Our teachers believed that it encouraged our mental development while teaching discipline and patience. They were right. Knitting is no longer a part of the school curriculum, but I believe knitting can be incredibly beneficial for children—it encourages creativity and coordination, and it helps stimulate the mind.

If you wish to ignite a love of knitting in your son or daughter, follow these tips. First, get them involved from the beginning; allow them to pick whatever yarn they like, and encourage them to take their time selecting it. Start them on a simple scarf. Don't worry about having them knit a gauge, just select the appropriate needles; make sure that the stitches are relatively big, and use a chunky yarn.

Cast on for them. Don't worry about teaching them how to cast on till they've mastered knitting and purling. Don't wait any longer than that, though—otherwise they'll think of casting on as a skill too difficult for them to master. Once they have the knack, keep a watchful eye, but don't hover over them. Knitting is an amazing way to help children develop a creative independence, but you'll need to give them their space in which to do so. Fix their big errors, but allow the little ones to slide, at least at first, and never rip out their work—unless they get to the stage where they are ambitious enough to want to rip out and reuse the yarn for another project.

Encourage boys by having them knit something for themselves, such as a wristband in an absorbent cotton. If you are inspired, you could even devise patterns for knee or elbow pads for them to wear while skateboarding. Just measure the circumference of their joints, calculate a gauge in a soft, chunky yarn, and show them how to knit the piece in a rib (to allow for the necessary elasticity).

KNITTING FOR CHARITY

Finally, consider spreading your love of knitting to those less fortunate than yourself. In recent years the number of volunteers who knit for hospitals, shelters for battered women and children and homeless people, and senior citizen homes has skyrocketed. Introducing knitting into these environments also brings companionship, creativity, and a sense of purpose—just like in a conventional knitting circle. I've heard stories of elderly people with Alzheimer's who can't remember their own names, or the faces of loved ones, but still remember how to knit. The needles and yarn conspire to bring back some crucial essence of who they once were—and what could be more of a blessing than that?

DAKOTA FANNING

A dedicated knitter since the age of seven, the lovely little movie star who packs quite a box-office punch, Dakota Fanning has become quite a voracious knitter. Dakota, who has a heart of gold, takes pride in knitting a scarf for each of her leading men, coming to me at my shop for advice. In her little voice, I hear "Edith, can you recommend a yarn that will hide my mistakes and something that will knit up fast?" To date, Dakota has quite a résumé of leading men sporting a Dakota original, among them Tom Cruise, Robert De Niro, and Denzel Washington. During her appearance on Oprah, *I watched with pride as she handed the talk-show diva a scarf I had helped her knit in my shop.*

Kellie Martin with Hedy Burress

Hedy Burress

Like the rest of the world, I was in a state of shock after 9/11. I wanted to do something but was unable to think of what. Finally I had an idea: create something unique and beautiful, and put it up for auction. I called every star who had ever walked into the store and asked them to knit a 6-by-6-inch afghan square. The response was so amazing that I had to make two afghans. Elizabeth Taylor, Debra Messing, Daryl Hannah, Sofia Coppola, Jennie Garth, Shelley Morrison, Bridget Fonda, Annette O'Toole, Justine Bateman, Tyra Banks, Julianne Moore, Caroline Rhea, Camryn Manheim, Tyne Daly, Antoinette Spolar-Levine, Nora Dunn, C. Thomas Howell, and Christopher Gorham were among the dozens of women and men who contributed. Some of the knitting was less than perfect—one Academy Award–winning star had two dropped stitches—but it was knitted with love and passion.

Even if you don't have celebrities to draw on, the patchwork blanket, made with dozens of small squares, is the perfect charity project. Find a women's shelter or child services organization that can accept your work, and knit it in washable, resilient

Shelley Morrison

yarns. Even if you never meet the recipients of your work, you'll know that they are grateful for it.

chapter seven

SIP & KNIT: PULL UP A CHAIR

". . . and have a seat, a glass of wine, perhaps some cheese and a taste of sweets. On any given day of the week, there are tons of women gathered around the table in my shop, happy to spend the time just knitting and socializing, while others visit to peruse the aisles and baskets overflowing with yarns and shop for the perfect project. It's like this all the time, and I'm on my feet running in all directions, helping one lady pick out hand-dyed yarns for a poncho, sitting at the table sketching a pattern for a sweater, teaching new knitters, and guiding others on more advance projects. There are days when I don't even have time to eat lunch or have a cup of coffee."

Then midweek everything seems to change, at least for a few hours. On Wednesday evenings La Knitterie Parisienne is open until 8:30 p.m.—or so reads the sign on the door. I'm usually there until 10 p.m.—but I'm not alone. On Wednesday evening, the shop is what I've coined "Sip & Knit" night. My clients come in droves, some direct from work, others wave to their husbands as they pass each other in their driveway.

Sip & Knit has evolved to become the coveted hour—or rather hours—in the knitting circle. One might wonder why these clients are stopping at the bakery, the cheese store, or the liquor store or hovering over their ovens just before they go to the knitting shop. It's because Wednesday evening at La Knitterie Parisienne is a social wine and cheese night, like Monday night football at the local bar, except much more refined. And, oh yeah, people also knit.

THE EVOLUTION OF SIP & KNIT

One of my clients is a wine connoisseur who frequently travels to Northern California wine country and decided to share her latest sampling with the group. She couldn't decide which one to bring in, so she brought one of each. The winos among us were delighted! The following week, someone else was inspired to bring a selection of cheeses and a warm baguette. The weekly sampling soon became a weekly must, and my clients began looking forward to this unique version of Wednesday night knitting. With a selection of French music piping in and homemade pastries and desserts added to the mix, Sip & Knit was officially born. By the time everyone packs up to go home, many are leaving with one bag more than they originally arrived with: their knitting, of course, and a doggie bag of treats.

ANNETTE O'TOOLE

One of my clients, Annette O'Toole, brought her husband with her one afternoon to show him the shop. I instantly recognized him. Michael McKean was Lenny in Laverne & Shirley. *I noticed Annette was clutching a magazine—and, in what I considered to be the ultimate compliment, she asked me to autograph the cover of the magazine, which I happened to be on.*

My open door policy at La Knitterie Parisienne is to make everyone feel welcome, and I do my best to make each and all feel comfortable and at home. While many of the Sip & Knit knitters have penciled Wednesday nights into their calendars, the evening continues to be La Knitterie Parisienne's late night, where anyone is welcome to shop, learn to knit, and even sip. One of my regulars and a favorite baking contributor to Sip & Knit is Nancy Schnoll, a young actress, whose desserts rival those of even the most accomplished bakers. Here are two delicious desserts that Nancy has shared with us at the shop.

"SIP & KNIT" RECIPES

Pecan Triangles

CRUST

¼ pound unsalted butter

3 cups all-purpose flour

1 egg

1 cup sugar

¼ teaspoon salt

¼ teaspoon baking powder

¼ cup whole milk

CREAM SUGAR AND BUTTER. Add egg and milk and the dry ingredients. Grease two cookie sheets (with edges) with butter or a nonstick spray. Roll out dough on floured surface and press and stretch dough into place with fingers. Be sure to stretch dough up on the inside of the cookie sheet edges and distribute evenly. Poke several times with a fork. Bake 15–19 minutes at 350 degrees. The edges of the dough should be golden brown and the rest a light golden brown.

NOTE: This recipe should be doubled, but only use 1 ½ of it divided evenly between two cookie sheets. It freezes well for future use.

MIXTURE

1 pound unsalted butter

1 pound dark brown sugar

3 ounces honey

1 ounce maple syrup

1 teaspoon vanilla

2 pounds raw unsalted pecan halves

ARRANGE PECANS IN THE BAKED CRUSTS FACE UP, "stacking" them staggered in a single layer. Very little crust should be visible. Over medium heat, melt butter in a large pot on top of stove. Add sugar, honey, syrup, and vanilla and bring to a boil. Keep stirring while it comes to a boil and after. It will bubble a lot and come up to almost the top of the pot. Boil for about 10 minutes. Be sure the sugar has dissolved, but do not let the mixture burn. Take pot off heat and immediately pour the mixture over pecans and crust in a zigzag pattern going between the two sheets. It is best to cover all the pecans. Bake again for 15 minutes at 350 degrees. When done, the mixture should bubble lightly around the edges, but the cooking time should not exceed 15 minutes. Watch closely and make sure the pecans and caramel do not burn. Let cool and remove from the cookie sheets. Cut off all 4 edges and cut into strips (with piece horizontally) and then into squares. Finally cut each square in half diagonally to create triangles.

Mandel Bread

3 eggs

1 cup oil

1 teaspoon vanilla

1 cup sugar

3 cups plus 2 tablespoons flour

1 teaspoon baking powder

¼ teaspoon salt

½ bag (6 ounces) miniature semi-sweet chocolate chips

½ cup chopped walnuts

cinnamon and sugar (to sprinkle)

IN A LARGE BOWL, CREAM ALL INGREDIENTS TOGETHER BY HAND. Mix the liquids first (eggs, oil, and vanilla), then add the dry ingredients. Mix until smooth. Put chips in entire mixture or use a mixture of both nuts and chips. Shape the 3 rolls on a jelly-roll pan with edges. Mixture will be oily and easy to work with. Each roll should be the width of the pan horizontally. Sprinkle with cinnamon and sugar and bake at 350 degrees for 30–40 minutes. The bread should be dark brown on the bottom—not golden. Let cool for a moment and then with a wide spatula make ½-inch slices. The pieces will be crumbly, but this is normal. Turn them on one side. Sprinkle with cinnamon and sugar, then put the pan back in the oven for about 10 minutes so the pieces can brown again. You can turn the pieces an additional time to brown the other side, but this is not necessary.

Enjoy!

Wednesday Night at Sip and Knit at La Knitterie Parisienne's Round Table

chapter eight

KNITTING FOR OTHERS

It happens around the beginning of November, usually the first Saturday of the month. Merrill and I will look up and see a tide of new faces, all the same: worried eyes, puckered brows, hands desperately juggling through piles of yarn.

It's the holiday rush. People who blithely promised back in March to 'knit you your Christmas present' are suddenly realizing that they have seven weeks to deliver a pile of carefully thought out, lovingly knitted gifts. Here is my single rule about knitting for the holiday season: if you're reading this any later than August, it may be too late. But if you do have time, here are some gift ideas to consider.

FELTED BAGS

Felting has become widely popular. Felting involves knitting a piece of work, like a purse or slippers, and intentionally shrinking it by putting it through several hot, agitated machine wash cycles. Because you will be shrinking it, you'll need to make your original item at least 30 percent larger than normal. It will seem almost outlandishly large—slippers that might fit a giant, handbags that could tote a Great Dane instead of a Chihuahua. Two of my clients, twin sisters Cindy and Lindy, impressed me with their felting creativity. Rather than use the normal felting materials—worsted wool—they picked a handful of eyelash and other novelty yarns in a palette of pink and red. I suggested that they incorporate alternate rows of worsted wool with the novelty yarns. When they felted it, the effect was amazing. The wool felted as expected, but the eyelash yarns retained their distinctive style, and the novelty yarns gave the finished bag a wonderful visual punch. Pleased with their work, they plowed through numerous bags. Some other gift ideas are scarves, shawls, ponchos, and blankets.

DEBRA MESSING

Many of my celebrity clients find La Knitterie Parisienne to be a quiet, welcoming haven where they can just relax and be themselves. When my very famous Will & Grace star walked into my shop with her dog, Leila, her knitting project centered around making a little blue sweater for the dog. Leila came for several fittings and sat on the table like a real pro while I measured. Because Debra is allergic to many fibers, we were challenged to find one that could work well, was soft, and came in the powder blue she desired. We did, and Debra knit a lovely dog cape sweater in powder blue with white trim. Leila was fashion forward on all fours.

The Paint-Chip Palette Approach

Color preference is such a personal choice—and can present quite a challenge when you're knitting a gift for a friend. You may get a request for a sweater in "midnight blue," but how can you know for sure that "midnight blue" means the same thing to both of you? Rather than make the wrong choice, suggest they visit their local hardware and paint store and pick out three paint chips—one that matches exactly the color they want, along with two alternates. You've successfully eliminated the guesswork.

THE ULTIMATE KNITTING GIFT

If your friends and family are interested in knitting—why not teach them how? Figure out who among your circle of loved ones will really take to the craft, and put together a gift for them. Include large-size needles, ranging from 11 to 15, select two or three balls of yarn that you know will appeal to them, a simple scarf pattern, and a copy of this book. If they are out-of-town friends, you might consider casting on and knitting the first few rows to make it even easier for them. After all, the best knitting gift of all is sharing your knowledge of your craft with others.

I remember when Julianne first began to knit with me at my shop. She would come straight from the set of Jurassic Park: The Lost World *and was excited about making a baby blanket for her first child. At that time, she told me a secret, and I felt honored to be among those she trusted. I didn't break her confidence, and I still wouldn't, but now since the cat's out of the bag, it's okay to say that she confided in me when she told me that she was pregnant with her first child.*

chapter nine

THE FUTURE OF KNITTING

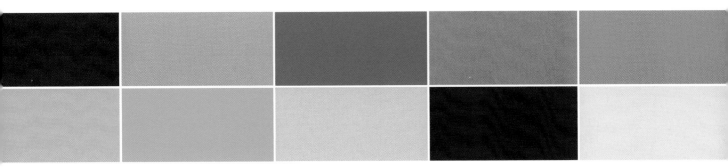

I can't wait to see how knitting continues to evolve.

In fact, one of the most exciting aspects of the

current knitting renaissance is witnessing how

knitters who have learned from me are melding

classic techniques and sophisticated stylings with

their own creativity.

If there is anything I hope that people take away from learning to knit with me, is that once you have a solid knowledge of the basic techniques, you have the power to explore a whole world of design and style.

All trends wax and wane in popularity, and knitting is no different. Twenty years ago needlepoint was all the rage, and everybody did it because it was the fashionable thing to do. A lot of those novelty needlepointers stopped, and many members of this new generation of knitters will stop as well, but the people who love knitting will stay with it.

I hope that you will become a knitter for whom knitting is more than just a passing whim. You may discover that knitting provides you with a meaningful form of self-expression, allows your creative juices to run wild, and benefits the people around you, while creating a legacy that conveys a little of who you are for your children and your children's children.

Like the meditative qualities of yoga, I hope that you'll find knitting to be a calming force as you navigate life's bumps and grinds, ups and downs, and that your new hobby will bring you a quiet space that is all your own—even if you are sitting on a commuter bus or surrounded by noisy children.

Most of all, I hope you will be inspired to pass on the art of knitting to your friends and family, and that you are always motivated to keep learning and developing your own skills. In this chapter I suggest ways in which you can keep your love of knitting alive. I haven't necessarily included patterns for the skills taught here, but they are easy to incorporate into existing designs or to experiment with in your own pattern writing.

USING YOUR IMAGINATION

One of the greatest benefits about the knitting circle at my shop is being exposed to the ideas and imaginations of dozens of men and women. As a shop owner, my role also includes teaching, but it's surprising how often I learn as well. Recently, a young knitter proudly came in to show

MARY-KATE AND ASHLEY OLSEN

The summer before Mary-Kate and Ashley headed to New York University, the sisters would frequent the shop. One afternoon, I *got a call from Ashley, who told me to buy the current issues of* People *and* In Touch *magazines. There was a picture of her* *walking along the beach toting my signature La Knitterie Parisienne bag.*

Mary is a talented actress in her early forties, tall, thin, striking, and the picture of health. The first time she came into the store she was panicked: her agent had booked her a commercial that was filming in two days, and she had to sit and knit on camera. Like any good actress she reassured the casting director that she was an old hand at knitting, then jumped in her car and came to see me. I taught her; she left, aced the commercial, and came back two days later.

The interesting part of the story is that when Mary first came in, she excused herself quite often to step outside for smoking breaks. As she continued to frequent the shop, I noticed that her smoking was beginning to decline. She confessed to me that for the first time in twenty years she was cutting down because her hands were now too busy with knitting to smoke. "Edith," she confided, "I knit throughout the day, and feel cranky and restless if I don't

get my knitting fix. But at least it's an addiction that's not going to kill me."

Mary's not the only one who's managed to overcome a difficult addiction. Everyone from nail biters to compulsive shoppers have replaced their more destructive habits with knitting. It's not always a perfect solution—my overshopper admits she spends almost as much on yarn as she did on clothes—but it's better than nothing.

me an item that she had knitted out of long strips of fabric she had cut herself. She was inspired by a jacket that I had made out of silk rippings, and I was equally impressed with the skirt she created. It's knitters like her that give me hope that knitting will remain an innovative and exciting craft, even when it's no longer as red hot as it is now.

Here are some advanced techniques that you should experiment with and consider using in your knitting. I picked these particular skills because they add shape, texture, style, and sophistication to your work. Two of these skills—short rows and updating vintage patterns—are tricky, but if you can master these concepts, they can unleash your creativity. You will become further inspired to customize your knitting and create truly personalized garments.

Have fun with these, and practice before you try to incorporate them into your knitting.

Short Rows.
The shaping technique known as short rows can be quite intimidating to beginners, and it does seem complex in theory. Essentially, it is a way of adding room to a knitted item by knitting backward and forward over the central stitches on a needle, while leaving the stitches at the beginning and end of the needle unknit. For instance,

Lisa Loeb came in because her brother was expecting a baby girl and she wanted to knit a little dress—in cashmere. I strongly recommend a blend—something more practical for a baby. But Lisa insisted on the

best and made a beautiful mocha-colored cashmere dress that her brother loved. Another time, Lisa invited me and Merrill to see her perform at the Getty Museum. During her opening monologue, she amused

the audience with anecdotes about herself and confided that one of her favorite pastimes is knitting. She went so far as to introduce me to the entire audience as her knitting guru.

a woman with a large bust might use short rows to add extra ease over her chest, and prevent the sweater from appearing shorter in the front than in the back. Once she has added enough room to make the sweater comfortable, she would knit to the end of the row, turn, and continue working her sweater as normal. She will still have the same number of stitches on her needles, and she will still be at the same point on her sweater (if she began the short row at 12 inches, her sweater will still be 12 inches long), but there will be "ease" across her chest where the extra rows are, and these extra rows will add another inch or so of depth to prevent the unattractive effect of the front being shorter than the back. If you want to add short rows to a simple sweater shape, knit to your bust, and add short rows over the middle, leaving about a fifth of your stitches untouched on either side. Use an existing sweater to help you calculate how many inches of depth you need to add.

Adding Texture to Your Knitting. One technique
to add a fun visual element to your knitting is the use of bobbles. Depending on how many stitches you work with, bobbles can be pea-size accents or bold golf ball–size design features. The former might enhance the border of a sweater, while the latter could be incorporated into a scarf design. Determine where in your pattern you would like to place the bobble. When you reach that stitch, knit into it five times. To do this, knit your stitch, but do not pull it off of your left-hand needle; instead keep bringing your needle forward and around to knit into the stitch again. When you have created five stitches out of one, turn your work and purl those five stitches, then turn again and knit and purl them again. Turn your work, knit two stitches together two times, pass it over, knit one stitch and pass it over, one stitch remains. Bobble is made.

Updating Vintage Sweaters. With the rise in knitting's popularity, vintage knitting pattern books from the 1920s on have resurfaced at flea markets, on the Internet, at garage sales, and even hidden in your grandmother's attic. While these patterns are still beautiful and continue to pass the test of time, the fit of these sweaters is outdated. With the vast selection of yarns now available, you can recreate a more modern and sophisticated version of the pattern you select. The tendency in those time periods was to knit with very small needles using yarns now considered medium gauge. The first step is to increase the size of your needles and to use a yarn of your choosing.

COPYING AN EXISTING SWEATER

At some point in their knitting lives most of my clients have come into the store clutching a picture ripped from the pages of the latest high fashion magazine. "Edith," they say, "I have to have this. Can't afford it, but have to have it." Though it might seem intimidating at first, it's quite easy to break down the essential design elements of an existing sweater and incorporate them into your work.

- Try to find a few different photos of the same garment. If it's a signature piece by a designer, it will probably be photographed by more than one magazine and from multiple angles. If you see it in a store, so much the better.

- Figure out what it is that you *love* about the sweater–the shape or the color, the stitch work or the style. You may well find that once you have isolated the things you like most about the sweater, you can leave off other design elements you don't care for as much.

- If you don't have the ability to recreate it on your own or your local knitting store doesn't offer that help and you don't happen to live near my shop, try this. Find an existing pattern that has a similar shape to the one you are copying and use that pattern as a launch pad for your own design. Use the techniques I described in chapter four to take your measurements and refine the pattern.

- Now, start knitting swatches, experiment with your design, and have fun with it. When you achieve a look that you like, work out your stitch and row gauge. If necessary, recalculate the pattern.

One of my knitting circle regulars came in with a picture of a chunky cashmere cardigan with cabling down each front half and a large hood. It was quite extravagant and so was the price. After we decided this was a must-have, we picked a yarn similar to the one in the magazine, and she knitted a gauge. Then I grabbed my tools of the trade: pen, calculator, and measuring tape. I made a sketch of the sweater and gave her the instructions, and she was on her way. Not only was the finished item made of a higher quality material than the original, but we were able to leave off the one thing she didn't like about the mass-produced sweater: the hood. In reconstructing this sweater, we had another advantage, because we were able to make it to the exact size, fit, and style that she desired.

Daryl Hannah

chapter ten

PATTERNS

It has been almost ten years since I opened La Knitterie Parisienne, and in that time I've taught thousands of knitters the same skills and techniques that you have mastered in my book. What I find most satisfying is to witness a knitter graduate from a nervous beginner—panicking at a dropped stitch and struggling to differentiate between a knit and a purl stitch—to a confident craftswoman who in turn passes her skills on to the beginner who comes and sits beside her at my knitting circle. I hope that you too will be inspired to share your knowledge and skills, and that the joy of knitting will be one with which you will carry throughout your life.

For many novice knitters, walking into a knitting store can be overwhelming and intimidating—observing the vast selections of yarns, the different choices in needles, and wondering if they dare sit down at a table full of laughing, chatting, rowdy women. Let alone join the more advanced knitters who rarely seem to even glance down at their projects as they chat and knit. At La Knitterie Parisienne, our goal is to create a friendly and welcoming environment so that both new and advanced

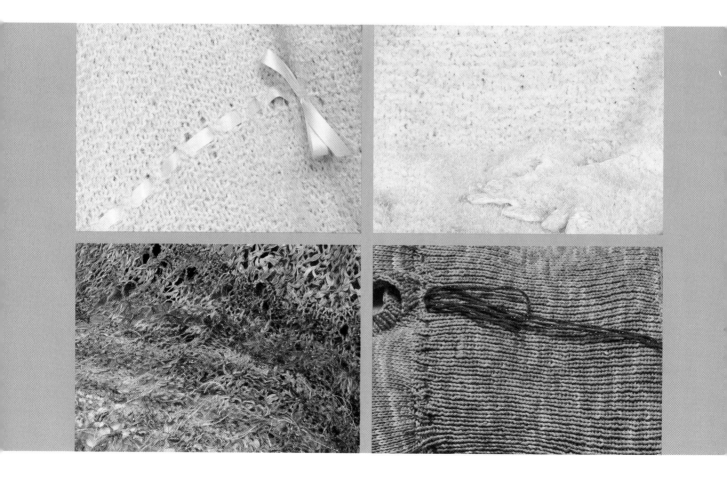

knitters are encouraged to learn and join other knitters who've come to make La Knitterie Parisienne their home away from home. La Knitterie Parisienne is the place where we make knitting fun, where strangers become friends, and where fabulous fashions are created. I hope you will find knitting as rewarding as I do.

The patterns in the following pages are organized in such a way as to guide you from simple designs, like a very easy scarf, to more challenging projects, among them a three-piece cashmere suit.

I've spent over two years designing and knitting these patterns, and I hope you enjoy knitting them as much as I enjoyed creating them for you.

[Simple and Beautiful Scarf]

MATERIAL

3 balls Noro Kureyon, same or assorted colors

4 balls Trendsetter Eyelash, black

NEEDLE

Size 13

STITCH

Garter = knit all rows

GAUGE

3 sts = 1"

FINISHED MEASUREMENT

8" × 72"

Cast on 24 sts with 1 strand of Kureyon and 1 strand of Eyelash held together. Knit in garter until desired length.

Bind off loosely.

I chose 3 different balls of Kureyon. Some colors ran from blue to pink, others from pink to green to purple. I wanted colors to run into each other in rainbow form.

Cut fringes 20" long.

Place 3 pieces in each fringe.

Antoinette Spolar Levine of
Curb Your Enthusiasm

[*Ribbon Scarf*]

Cast on 18 sts with 1 strand of Giotto and 1 strand of Eyelash held together.

Knit in garter to 70″ or desired length.

Bind off loosely.

Tip to bind off: Leave a piece of yarn 4 times the length of your desired width.

Finishing: Cut fringes approximately 20″ long. Fringes will be 10″ long.

Use 3 pieces of each yarn for fringes.

MATERIAL
1 ball Colinette Giotto
2 balls Trendsetter Eyelash
1 ball Katia Scala for fringes

NEEDLE
Size 17

GAUGE
2.25 sts = 1″

STITCH
Garter

FINISHED MEASUREMENT
8″ × 70″

[*Very* Sex and the City *Scarf*]

MATERIAL	6 balls Trendsetter Bloom
NEEDLE	Size 35
GAUGE	1.75 sts = 1″
FINISHED MEASUREMENT	8″ × 80″

Yarn is used double throughout.

Cast on 14 sts.

Knit 8 rows in garter.

* Knit 1 row wrapping yarn 3× around both needles, knit 6 rows. * Repeat from * to * until desired length.

Finish with knit 8 rows instead of 6 rows.

Bind off loosely.

Cut 22″ fringe strands to make actual fringe size 11″ in length.

Place 4 pieces in each fringe.

Anel Lopez Gorham of *Popular*

[Lost in Translation *Scarf*]

Cast on 26 sts.

ROW 1: K1, * YO, K1 * repeat from * across the row to last st, K1.

ROW 2: K1, purl across to last st, end with K1.

ROW 3: K1, * K2tog * repeat across the row, end with K1.

ROW 4: K1, * YO, K2tog * repeat from * end with K1.

ROW 5: K1, * YO, K2tog * repeat from * end with K1.

ROW 6: Knit across.

ROW 7: Knit across.

Repeat from Rows 1 through 7 until desired length.

Bind off loosely.

MATERIAL		
3 balls Rowan Kid Classic		
NEEDLE		
Size 7		
GAUGE		
3.70 sts = 1″		
FINISHED MEASUREMENT		
7″ × 70″		

J. Robin Miller of *General Hospital*

Audrey Eig

[*Fiori Scarf*]

MATERIAL

4 balls Skacel Fiori

(4 colors that complemented each other were used)

NEEDLE

Size 17

GAUGE

1.80 sts = 1″

STITCH

Dropped garter
Garter

FINISHED MEASUREMENT

8.5″ × 80″

ROW 1: Knit 1 st wrapping yarn around needle 3×.

ROW 2: Knit 1 st dropping extra loop.

To ensure you have enough for your fringes, cut fringes before you start your work. Cut 22″ fringe strands to make actual fringe size 11″ in length.

With color 1 cast on 15 sts.

Knit 5 rows in garter.

ROW 1: Knit 1 st * knit wrapping yarn 3× around one needle, repeat from * end with K1.

ROW 2: Knit across dropping extra loops.

ROWS 3 through 5: Knit across.

Change to second color.

Repeat Rows 1 through 5.

Change to third color.

Repeat Rows 1 through 5.

Change to fourth color.

Repeat Rows 1 through 5.

Knit 5 rows in garter.

Bind off loosely.

FINISHING

Place your fringes.

[Scarf in Pink Cashmere and Rabbit Fur]

Scarf in Pink Cashmere and Rabbit Fur

MATERIAL

5 skeins Classic Elite Forbidden

5 yards rabbit fur

1 package round stitch markers

NEEDLE

Size 15

GAUGE

3 sts = 1"

STITCH

Seed stitch

Twisted rib

FINISHED MEASUREMENT

8" × 72" or desired length

Yarn is used double throughout.

Cast on 24 sts. Proceed as follows:

ROW 1: Knit 4 sts in seed, place marker. * Knit 2nd st on left needle by going in back of 1st st. Do not remove from needle. Knit 1st st, then remove both sts from needle. Knit 2nd st by going in front of 1st st, knit 1st st, and remove both at the same time. * Repeat from * to * to the last 4 sts. Place marker, knit 4 sts in seed.

ROW 2: Knit 4 sts in seed. Purl across. Knit 4 sts in seed.

After 4 rows of pattern, work 2 rows of rabbit fur in pattern.

Continue repeating rows 1 and 2 with Forbidden only to desired length.

Reverse fur placement before the last 4 rows of your work.

Bind off loosely in pattern.

Shellie Kleinman

[*Reversible Scarf for the Man in Our Life*]

Cast on 27 sts.
Proceed as follows:

ROW 1: * K2, P2 * P1. (This pattern will form the mistake rib.)

ROW 2: Same as Row 1.

Repeat until desired length.

Bind off loosely.

MATERIAL	
3 skeins Noro Iro or Big Kureyon	
NEEDLE	
Size 11	
GAUGE	
3 sts = 1″	
STITCH	
Mistake rib	
FINISHED MEASUREMENT	
9″ × 70″	

Christopher Gorham of *Medical Investigation*

Natalie Eig

[*Le Rouge et le Noir Scarf**]

MATERIAL
4 balls Mondial Kross
1 ball Gedifra Calista
1 ball Schachenmayr Pompon

NEEDLE
Size 13

GAUGE
3.25 sts = 1"

FINISHED MEASUREMENT
8" × 74"

Cast on 26 sts with 1 strand of Calista and 1 strand of Pompon. Knit in garter for 4". Increase 2 sts across the last row = 28 sts. Change to pattern and Kross as follows:

ROW 1: K1, P1 through back loop (henceforth tbl), K1 * P2, K1, P1 tbl, K1 * repeat from * across the row.

ROW 2: P1, K1 tbl, P1 * K1, YO, K1, P1, K1 tbl, P1 * repeat from * across the row.

ROW 3: K1, P1 tbl, K1 * P3, K1, P1 tbl, K1 * repeat from * across the row.

ROW 4: P1, K1 tbl, P1 * K3, pass 2 sts over the 1st (PSSO), P1, K1 tbl, P1 * repeat from * across the row.

Repeat rows 1 through 4. Knit to 70" or desired length.

Change to 1 strand of Calista and 1 strand of Pompon, decrease 2 sts evenly.

Knit 4" in garter.

Bind off loosely.

*Red and Black Scarf

[Le Rouge et le Noir Hat*]

MATERIAL

1 ball Mondial Kross
1 ball Gedifra Calista
1 ball Schachenmayr Pompon

NEEDLE

Size 13

GAUGE

3.25 sts = 1"

STITCH

Garter

FINISHED MEASUREMENT

22"

Cast on 63 sts with 1 strand of Pompon and 1 strand of Calista. Knit in garter for 1". Increase 5 sts across the last row (68 sts).

Change to Kross and proceed in pattern as follows (pattern is a multiple of 5 + 3 sts):

ROW 1: K1, P1 through back loop (tbl). K1 * P2, K1, P1 tbl, K1 * repeat from * to * across the row.

ROW 2: P1, K1 tbl, P1 * K1, YO, K1, P1, K1 tbl, P1 * repeat from * to * across the row.

ROW 3: K1, P1 tbl, K1 * P3, K1, P1 tbl, K1 * repeat from * to * across the row.

ROW 4: P1, K1 tbl, P1 * K3, pass 2 sts over the 1st (PSSO), P1, K1 tbl, P1 * repeat from * to * across the row.

Work in pattern until the hat measures 8". Knit 1 row decreasing 10 sts evenly (58 sts).

Purl 2 sts together across the row (29 sts). Cut yarn leaving a tail long enough to sew seam down the side. Thread a yarn needle. Pull through all remaining sts on needle, tighten up. Pull yarn around circle formed by tightened sts, fasten up, and sew seam.

*Red and Black Hat

[*Hat in Aura and Zucca*]

MATERIAL

1 ball each, Trendsetter Zucca
and Aura

1 ball Bouton D'Or Dune

1 package stitch markers

NEEDLE

Size 10½ circular 16″

GAUGE

2.25 sts = 1″

**FINISHED
MEASUREMENT**

22″

Cast on 50 sts with Zucca. Place marker. Join, taking care not to twist your sts.

K1, P1 rib for 3 rows.

Continue in garter for 1″. (When you knit in the round garter becomes stockinette.)

Change to 1 strand of Zucca and 1 strand of Aura, purl for 3 rows.

Change to Zucca, knit for 3 rows.

Change to 1 strand of Bouton D'Or Dune and 1 strand of Aura, purl for 6 rows.

Change to Zucca, knit for 2″.

Change to Aura and Bouton D'Or Dune * P2tog * repeat to end. Repeat this round one time more.

Cut yarn leaving a 10″ tail. Thread a yarn needle, pull through all remaining sts on needle one at a time, tighten up, and fasten off.

[Angora Super Hat]

Cast on 84 sts. Place marker. Join, taking care not to twist your sts.

K1, P1 rib for 4 rows or ½".

Continue in seed stitch until piece measures 5".

Divide work in 4 quarters of 21 sts each.

Work each triangle separately as follows:

Working on first 21 sts. Place remaining 3 quarters on stitch holders.

K2tog at each end of row until 1 st remains.

Repeat on each of three remaining triangles. Then K2tog sts 2× and bind off.

Sew seams with mattress stitch.

MATERIAL		
2 balls Anny Blatt Angora Super		
3 stitch holders		
1 package stitch markers		

NEEDLE
Size 8 circular 16"

GAUGE
4 sts = 1"

STITCH
Rib: K1, P1
Seed stitch

FINISHED MEASUREMENT
21"

107

Nancy Schnoll, actress

[*Furry Shrug*]

MATERIAL

2 balls Trendsetter Willow

2 balls Gedifra Tecno Hair

2 balls DK Cotton (110 yards each ball)

NEEDLES

Size 17

Crochet hook, size L

GAUGE

2 sts = 1"

STITCH

Stockinette

FINISHED MEASUREMENT

18" × 44"

Yarn is used triple throughout, with one strand of each.

Cast on 36 sts.

Work in stockinette until piece measures 44".

Bind off loosely.

Sew seams 11" on each end of piece for armhole shaping. With 2 strands of cotton, single crochet all around body of shrug.

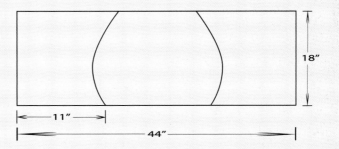

Carolyn Hennesy of
Curb Your Enthusiasm

[*Pink Mohair Capelet*]

MATERIAL

8 balls Katia Ingenua

NEEDLES

Size 11 and 13

GAUGE

3 sts = 1″

STITCH

Stockinette: Knit 1 row (RS), purl 1 row (WS)

Reverse: Purl 1 row on right side, knit 1 row on wrong side

Rib: K1, P1

FINISHED MEASUREMENT

42″ × 16″

Yarn is used double throughout.

Cast on 126 sts on size 13 needles.

* Knit 10 rows in stockinette, knit 3 rows in reverse stockinette. * Repeat from * to * 5×.

When piece measures 16″ finish with 4 rows of stockinette.

With size 11 needles pick up 48 sts on the narrow part of your work.

Next row: K2tog across the row = 24 sts.

Next row: K2tog across the row = 12 sts.

K1, P1 pattern for 8″.

Repeat pick-up process on other side.

FINISHING

Single crochet around entire piece. Follow with one row of reverse crochet or crab stitch. Select closure of choice.

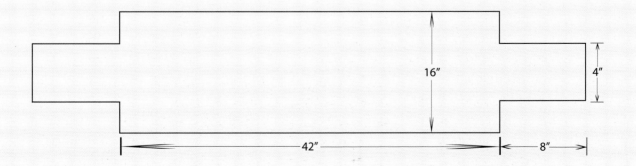

16″

4″

42″

8″

[*Poncho in Cashmere*]

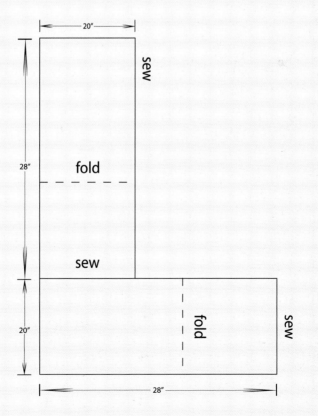

MATERIAL

6 skeins Noro Canna cashmere

NEEDLES

Size 15

Size 13 circular 16"

Crochet hook, size L

GAUGE

2.50 sts = 1"

STITCH

Stockinette

Garter

Seed stitch

Double wrap, wrapping yarn around both needles

FINISHED MEASUREMENT

20" × 28"

Make 2 pieces alike.

With size 15 needles cast on 50 sts. Work 14 rows in stockinette, 3 rows in seed stitch, 2 rows in garter, 1 row in double wrap, 2 rows in garter. Continue in stockinette until piece measures 28".

Bind off loosely.

With circular size 13 needles, pick up and knit 64 sts around the neck. K1, P1 for 1½". Bind off loosely in pattern.

Single crochet around entire piece.

FINISHING

See diagram.

Cut 14" pieces for fringes; use 3 pieces for each fringe.

Leo

[Baby Blanket #1]

MATERIAL

4 balls Sirdar Funky Fur

3 balls Sirdar Snowflake Chunky

2 balls Katia Ola

NEEDLES

Size 15

Crochet hook, size K

GAUGE

2 sts = 1"

STITCH

Garter

Single crochet

Crochet shell

FINISHED MEASUREMENT

36" × 38"

Cast on 72 sts with 1 strand each of Funky Fur and Snowflake Chunky. Work in garter for 38".

Bind off loosely.

FINISHING

With Ola work 1 row of single crochet (sc) followed by 1 row of crochet shell * 1 double crochet in first sc 5× in the same st, 3 sc in next 3 sts * repeat all around the blanket.

Semara Lapchinski

Baby Blanket with Ruffle

MATERIAL

630 yards worsted cotton

7 balls Lang Furore or Gedifra Tecno Hair

4 balls Trendsetter Segue

NEEDLES

Size 15

Crochet hook, size K

GAUGE

2.75 sts = 1″

STITCH

Stockinette

Reverse stockinette

Seed stitch: K1, P1.
Reverse on second row: P1, K1.
If a knit faces you, purl it.

FINISHED MEASUREMENT

36″ × 38″

With 1 strand of each yarn together cast on 100 sts.

Knit in stockinette for 4¾″.

Change to reverse stockinette for 4¾″.

Change to stockinette for 4¾″.

Work in seed stitch for 4¾″.

Change to stockinette for 4¾″.

Work in seed stitch for 4¾″.

Change to stockinette for 4¾″.

Change to reverse stockinette for 4¾″.

Bind off loosely.

FINISHING

With Trendsetter Segue * single crochet (sc) in next 3 sts, skip 1 * repeat to end. Put 3 sc in each corner st.

FOR RUFFLE

Double crochet 5× in each st all around.

Carnie Wilson, singer

[*Diaper Bag with Changing Pad*]

MATERIAL

19 balls Tahki Chat–navy
9 balls Tahki Chat–green
4 snaps
1 separating zipper
Waterproof fabric
1 package stitch markers

NEEDLES

Size 10 and 13

GAUGE

3 sts = 1″
3½ rows = 1″

STITCH

Garter
Stockinette

FINISHED MEASUREMENT

14″ × 18″

Yarn is used double throughout.

BODY OF BAG

Cast on 70 sts with 2 strands of navy yarn and size 13 needle. Knit 8 sts, place marker. Knit 54 sts, place marker, knit 8 sts.

Keeping the first and last 8 sts in garter, proceed in stockinette on the middle 54 sts until piece measures 14″.

Bind off 8 sts at beginning of next 2 rows.

Work in stockinette for 5″.

Cast on 8 sts at beginning of next 2 rows. Proceed as before until piece measures 14″ from the cast-on row of 8 sts.

Bind off loosely.

FLAP

With double green yarn pick up and knit 53 sts on the center sts of the cast-on row.

Decrease 1 st each end of every other row 9×.

Work until flap measures 5½″.

Bind off remaining 35 sts.

CHANGING PAD

With size 13 needle and 2 strands of yarn in navy cast on 110 stitches.

Proceed as follows:

ROW 1: Knit 33 sts, slip 1 st, K36, slip 1 st, K39.

ROW 2: Purl all stitches.

Repeat rows 1 and 2 until piece measures 17″.

Bind off loosely.

TAB

Make 2 pieces alike.

With size 10 needles and double yarn in green cast on 8 sts.

Knit in garter for 4½".

Bind off loosely.

POCKET

With size 13 needles and double yarn in green cast on 56 sts.

Work in garter for 2 rows.

Proceed as follows:

K5, slip 1 st, K44, slip 1 st, K5.

Keeping the first and last 4 sts in garter, proceed in stockinette until piece measures 11½", then continue in garter on all sts for 6 rows.

Bind off loosely.

HANDLE

With size 10 needles cast on 12 sts in blue and 13 sts in green.

ROW 1: Knit in garter as follows: K12, slip 1 st, K12.

ROW 2: Knit across.

Repeat rows 1 and 2 until piece measures 29".

Bind off loosely.

SIDE POCKETS

Make 2 pieces alike.

Cast on 23 sts.

ROW 1: K4, slip 1 st, K13, slip 1 st, K4.

Keeping the first and last 4 sts in garter, continue on the center 13 sts in stockinette until pockets measure 8½", then knit 6 rows in garter.

Bind off loosely.

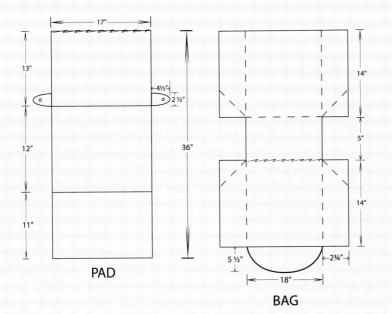

PAD

BAG

FINISHING

Sew pockets, fold handle in half, sew together.

Sew zipper to the outside front of bag and the bottom of changing pad.

Sew tabs.

Line bag and pad with washable vinyl. I suggest purchasing a colorful vinyl outdoor tablecloth.

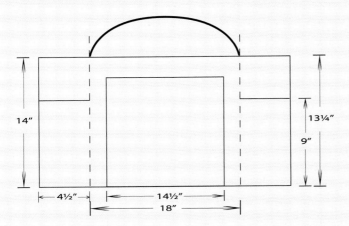

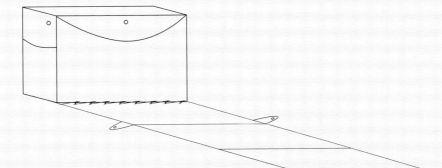

Mary Wall, actress

[Raffia Bag with Bamboo Handles]

MATERIAL

8 balls Mondial Paglia
di Firenze

1 set bamboo handles

NEEDLES

Size 11

Crochet hook, size I

GAUGE

3.5 sts = 1″

**FINISHED
MEASUREMENT**

12″ × 14″

Make 2 pieces alike for front and back.

Yarn is used double throughout.

With 2 strands of raffia cast on 48 sts.

Work the same for front and back.

Proceed as follows:

ROW 1 (WS): Purl.

ROW 2 (RS): Knit.

ROW 3: Purl.

ROW 4: * K2tog through back loop 2×, YO K1, 4×, K2tog through back loop 2× * Repeat to end.

Repeat rows 1 through 4 for pattern until piece measures 12″ or desired length.

Knit in stockinette for 1″. Purl 1 row on right side. Knit in stockinette for 1″. This is the part to be folded over the bamboo handles.

Bottom crochet shell: Double crochet in the same st, 6×, 2 sc, sc in next 2 sts * (* repeat to end.)

FINISHING

Sew pieces together.

Lining optional.

[*Shrug in Angora*]

MATERIAL

3 balls Anny Blatt
Angora Super

4 balls Anny Blatt Victoria

NEEDLES

Size 7 and 11

Crochet hook, size H

STITCH

Rib: K1, P1

Stockinette

GAUGE

3.5 sts = 1″

**FINISHED
MEASUREMENT**

13″ × 56″

With size 7 needles cast on 46 sts with Victoria. Work in K1, P1 rib for 2½″.

Change to size 11 needles and add 1 strand of Angora Super to the Victoria, work in stockinette for 53½″ or desired length.

Change to Victoria only and size 7 needles, work in rib (K1, P1) for 2½″.

Bind off loosely in pattern.

FINISHING

Sew seams to underarms.

Single crochet around shrug with 2 strands of Victoria.

[*Garden Party Shawl*]

MATERIAL
5 balls Bouton D'Or Angora 70
4 balls Karabella Magic
2 balls Stacy Charles Twist
1 ball Artful Cinema

NEEDLE
Size 11 circular 40″

GAUGE
2¼ sts = 1″

STITCH
Garter

FINISHED MEASUREMENT
16″ × 70″

Cast on 160 sts with 1 strand of Angora 70 and 1 strand of Magic. Knit 2 rows in garter. Proceed in pattern as follows:

* K10, K10 wrapping 2× around needle. * Repeat from * to * across the row.

* P10, dropping extra loop and wrapping again, P10. * Repeat from * to * across the row.

Knit 4 rows in garter. * K10 wrapping 2× around needle, K10. * Repeat from * to * across the row.

* P10, P10 dropping extra loop and wrapping again. * Repeat from * to * across the row.

Knit 4 rows in garter. Proceed in this manner until piece measures 16″. Knit 2 rows in garter, binding off loosely.

Cut fringes using Twist and Cinema, 22″ long.

Emma Tank

[*Emma Tank*]

BACK

Cast on 50 (55, 60) sts.

Work in K5, P5 rib for 2". Decrease 1 st for size 38 and start double moss stitch pattern until piece measures 12" (12", 13").

ARMHOLE SHAPING

Bind off 3 sts at beginning of next 2 rows.

Bind off 2 sts at beginning of next 2 rows.

K2tog at beginning and end of needle every other row 1× (3×, 5×).

When armhole measures 8" (8", 8½") put all sts on stitch holder.

FRONT

Proceed as for back until armhole measures 4".

Put center 10 sts on stitch holder.

Attach another ball of yarn, at neck edge and every other row.

Bind off 3 sts 1×.

Bind off 2 sts 2×.

K2tog 1×.

When armhole measures same as back put all sts on stitch holder.

FINISHING

Armhole and neck:

Single crochet 3 sts in a row, skip 1. Continue all around.

Follow with a row of reverse crochet.

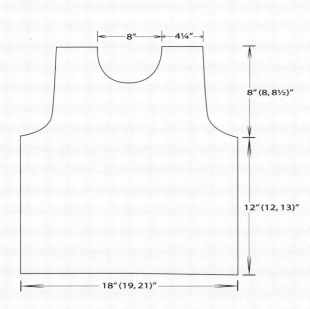

French Boatneck Sweater

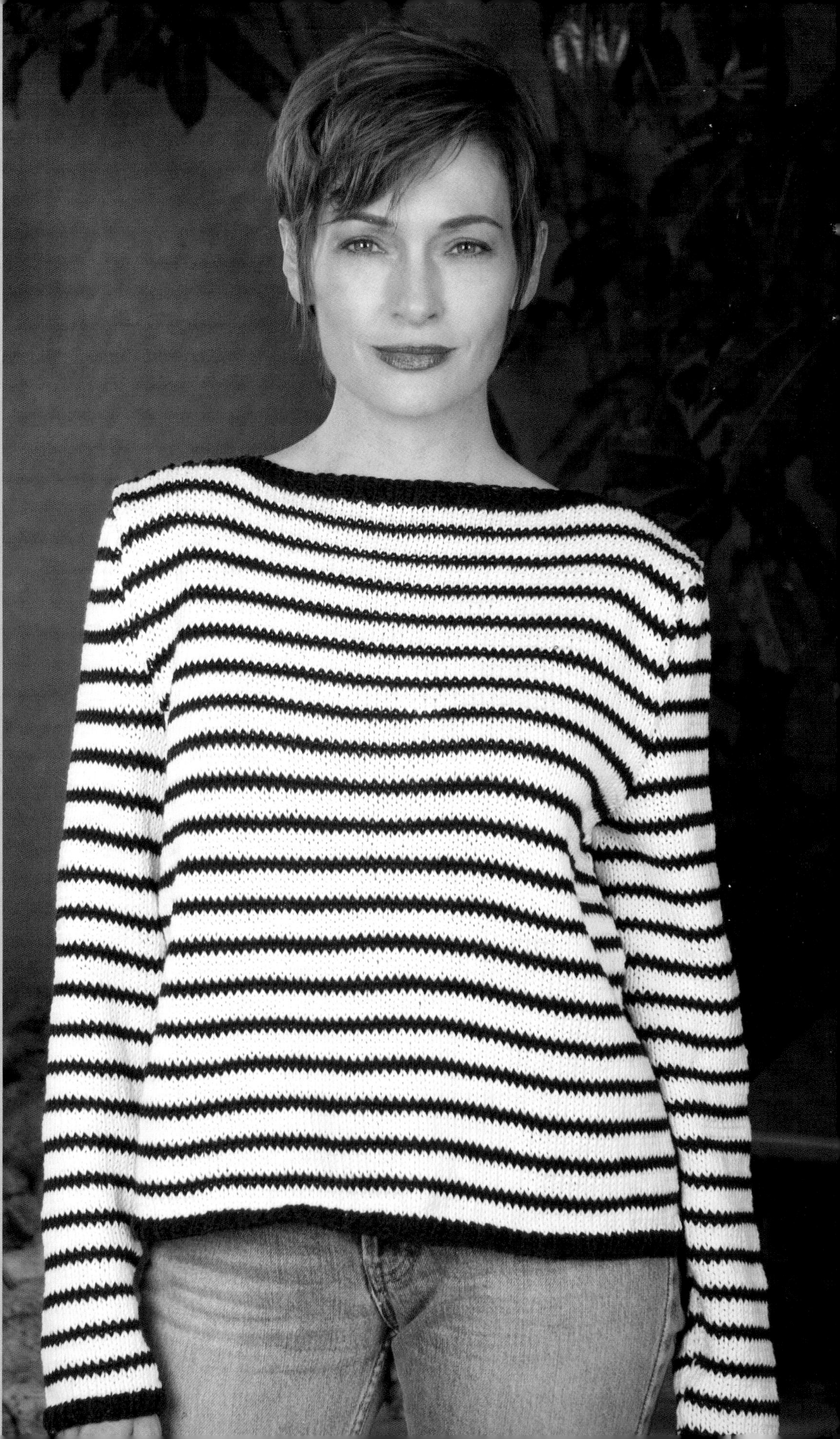

[*French Boatneck Sweater*]

MATERIAL

OnLine Clip 4 (5) balls white,
2 balls navy

2 stitch holders

NEEDLE

Size 8

GAUGE

5 sts = 1″

6 rows = 1″

STITCH

Stockinette
4 rows white, 2 rows blue

**FINISHED
MEASUREMENT**

Size 38 (42, 46)

Make two pieces alike for front and back.

Cast on 94 (106, 116) sts in navy.

K1, P1 rib for 4 rows.

Change to white and work in stockinette until piece measures 12″ (13″, 14″) or desired length. Do not cut yarn when changing colors; twist and carry the colors on the side of your work when changing colors.

Shape armholes. Bind off 5 sts at beginning of next 2 rows.

Bind off 2 sts at beginning of next 2 rows.

K2tog at each end of every other row 5× (8×, 9×). 70 (76, 78) sts remain.

When armhole measures 7¾″ (7¾″, 8¼″) change to navy, K1, P1 rib for ¾″. When armhole measures 8½″ (8½″, 9″), put all remaining sts on stitch holder.

SLEEVES

Cast on in navy 40 (42, 44) sts.

K1, P1 rib for 4 rows.

Change to stockinette and white. Increase 1 st at each end of needle every 7th (6th, 5th) row 10× (12×, 13×).

When sleeve measures 17½″ (18½″, 19½″) or desired length bind off 5 sts at beginning of next 2 rows.

Bind off 2 sts at beginning of next 2 rows.

K2tog at each end of needle every other row 9× (12×, 14×).

When cap measures 5½″ (5½″, 6″) bind off 2 sts at beginning of next 2 rows.

Bind off 3 sts at beginning of next 2 rows.

Bind off remaining 18 sts at once.

FINISHING

Weave loose ends.

Put shoulders together with a three-needle bind-off.

Leaving a 9″ opening for neck.

HINT

Place safety pin in the middle of the back to mark beginning of armhole bind-off.

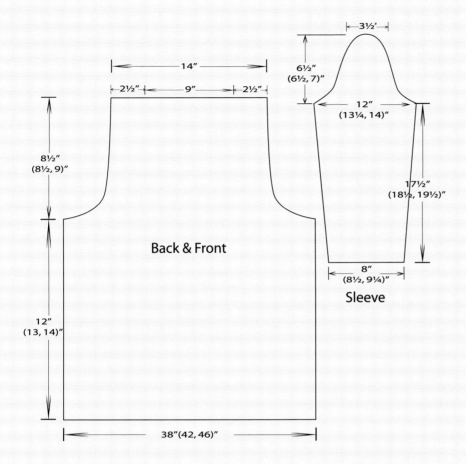

Back & Front

14"

2½" 9" 2½"

8½"
(8½, 9)"

12"
(13, 14)"

38"(42, 46)"

3½"

6½"
(6½, 7)"

12"
(13¼, 14)"

Sleeve

17½"
(18½, 19½)"

8"
(8½, 9¼)"

[*Dress in Segue*]

MATERIAL

4 balls Trendsetter Segue

Stitch holder

NEEDLE

Size 19

GAUGE

1.90 sts = 1″

2 rows = 1″

STITCH

Garter

Pattern A: K1 row wrapping 2×

K1 row dropping extra loop

Pattern B: P1 * YO, P2tog *
repeat from *, end with P1

Pattern C: K1 * YO, K2tog *
repeat from *

**FINISHED
MEASUREMENT**

Size 38/40

Back/Front

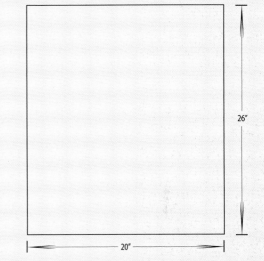

Front and back are alike.

Cast on 36 sts.

Work in garter for 4 rows.

Work 8 rows of pattern A.

Work 4 rows of garter.

Work 8 rows of pattern B.

Work 4 rows of garter.

Work 8 rows of pattern C.

Work 4 rows of garter.

Work 8 rows of pattern A.

Work 4 rows of garter.

Put all sts on stitch holder.

Sleeve

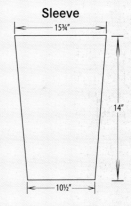

SLEEVES

Cast on 20 sts.

Work in garter for 4 rows.

* Work 4 rows of pattern A.

Work 4 rows of garter *.

Increase 1 st at each end of needle on the first row of garter every time you change your pattern. Repeat this increase 5×. When sleeve measures 14″ bind off loosely.

FINISHING

Join shoulder seams with a three-needle bind-off, leaving a 9″ opening for neck. Sew seams. Tie with a bow on each shoulder if desired.

[*Tank Top with Feather Trim*]

MATERIAL

9 balls Noro Cashmel

1½ yds Lang Piuma

2 medium stitch holders

NEEDLES

Size 7

Size 5 circular 24″

Crochet hook, size F

GAUGE

5½ sts = 1″

7 rows = 1″

FINISHED MEASUREMENT

Size 38

Make two pieces alike.

Multiple of 6 + 2.

ROW 1 (Right Side): P2 * K1 through back loop (tbl), K1, P1, K1 tbl, P2. Repeat from * to end.

ROW 2: K2 * P1 tbl, K1, P1, K1 tbl, K2. Repeat from * to end.

ROW 3: P2 * K1 tbl, P1, K1, K1 tbl, P2. Repeat from * to end.

ROW 4: K2 * P1 tbl, P1, K1, P1 tbl, K2. Repeat from * to end.

Repeat these 4 rows for pattern.

With size 7 needles cast on 104 sts and work in pattern until piece measures 13″. Bind off 6 sts at beginning of next 2 rows, then every other row K2tog at each end of needle 9×. When armhole measures 4″ put all sts on holder.

FINISHING

With size 5 needles pick up and knit 74 sts from first holder. Cable cast on 26 sts. Pick up and knit 74 sts from second holder. Cable cast on 26 sts. You should now have 200 sts.

K1, P1 rib for 1″. Bind off loosely in pattern. Single crochet around each armhole. Sew Piuma around neck. Sew side seams.

[*Poncho*]

MATERIAL

7 balls Lang Roma
1 package markers

NEEDLES

Size 13 circular 40″
Crochet hook, size J

GAUGE

2.75 sts = 1″

With size 13 circular needles, cast on 260 sts.

Knit 1 row, then join. (Be careful not to twist sts.)

Place marker of a different color to mark beginning of row. Do not increase before or after this marker.

Knit 32 sts, place marker. * Knit 65 sts, place marker. * Repeat 2× more, finish with knit 33 sts.

Knit 2 rows.

Decrease as follows:

K2 sts before marker. Slip 1, K1, PSSO, after marker K2tog.

Repeat every 3rd row until 57 sts remain.

Bind off loosely.

FINISHING

Single crochet around neck (* 3 sc, skip 1 st * repeat to end).

Next row crab stitch or reverse crochet in every stitch.

FRINGES

Cut pieces 22″ long. Place 3 pieces for each fringe ¾″ apart.

HINT

Cast on with 2 balls of yarn. Place markers every 20 sts to make
the counting process easier.

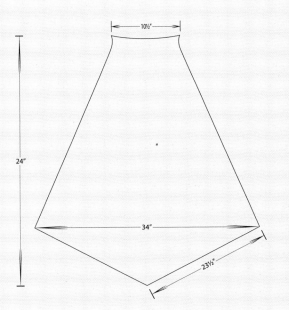

[*Tank*]

MATERIAL

4 balls Lang Roma

NEEDLES

Size 11 circular 16″

Size 13

Crochet hook, size H

GAUGE

2.75 sts = 1″

4 rows = 1″

STITCH

Mistake rib. Using odd number of sts, always repeat this row for pattern. K2, P2 across the row. Finish with 1 st.

FINISHED MEASUREMENT

Size 34 (38, 40)

BACK

Cast on 47 (53, 55) sts.

Work in mistake rib for 2″.

Start pattern as follows:

Change to stockinette.

ROW 1: K1 st, P45 (51, 53), end with K1.

ROW 2: P1 st, K45 (51, 53), end with P1.

ROW 3: K2, P43 (49, 51), end with K2.

Increase the stockinette side by replacing the purl in the center 26× until 1 st remains in purl in the center.

Continue in stockinette, knit on right side, purl on wrong side on all sts.

When piece measures 12″ from beginning shape armhole:

Bind off 3 sts at beginning of next 2 rows.

Bind off 2 sts at beginning of next 2 rows.

K2tog at each end of needle every other row 5×. When armhole measures 8½″ put all remaining sts on stitch holder.

FRONT

Proceed as back until armhole measures 5½″.

Put the center 11 sts on holder.

Attach another ball of yarn.

At neck edge and every other row bind off 2 sts 2×.

K2tog 2×.

When piece measures same as back put all sts on holder.

FINISHING

Neck: With size 11 circular 16″ pick up 57 sts.

Knit in the round in stockinette until neck measures 2″.

Change to mistake rib for 4 rows.

Knit in the round for 3 rows.

Bind off loosely.

ARMHOLE

One row of single crochet all around followed with one row of reverse crochet.

HINT

Turn stitch holder upside down to prevent stitches from falling off in case holder opens up.

Tank

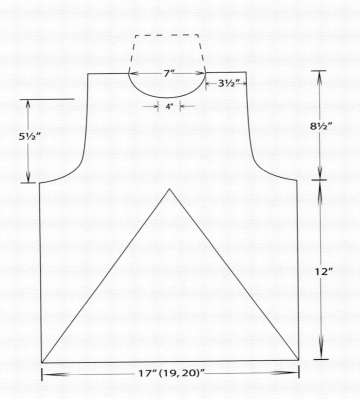

[*Jacket*]

MATERIALS

8 balls Anny Blatt
Angora Super

8 balls Anny Blatt Victoria

5 buttons

5 stitch holders

NEEDLES

Size 11

Crochet hook, size H

GAUGE

3.30 sts = 1″

4 rows = 1″

STITCH

Stockinette

Twisted rib

ROW 1: K2, P2

ROW 2: P2, K2

ROW 3: Knit second st by
passing in back of first, then
remove both at the same time

ROW 4: P2, K2

FINISHED
MEASUREMENT

Size 36 (40)

BACK

With 1 strand of Angora Super and 1 strand of Victoria together, cast on 60 (69) sts.

Knit in stockinette until piece measures 12″ (13″).

Bind off 4 sts at beginning of next 2 rows.

Bind off 2 sts at beginning of next 2 rows.

K2tog at each end of needle every other row 1× (5×).

When armhole measures 8½″ put all sts on stitch holder.

FRONT

Cast on 30 (35) sts, work in stockinette.

Mark pocket at 5½″ from beginning 9 sts from front edge on 17 sts.

Continue until piece measures 12″ (13″).

Bind off and decrease for armhole, but on 1 side only.

At the same time, at 13″ (14″) mark the second pocket 9 sts from front edge, but on 13 sts only.

When armhole measures 5½″ at neck edge bind off 6 sts 1×. Then every other row bind off 2 sts 1×, K2tog 4×.

When armhole measures same as back put all sts on holder.

Make another front reversing shaping and omitting front top pocket.

SLEEVES

Cast on 30 (34) sts, work in stockinette.

Increase 1 st at each end of needle every 10th row 6× (every 7th row 7×) = 42 sts (48 sts).

When sleeve measures 16″ (17″) bind off 4 sts at beginning of next 2 rows.

Bind off 2 sts at beginning of next 2 rows.

K2tog at each end of needle every other row 4× (7×).

When cap measures 6″ bind off 2 sts at beginning of next 2 rows.

Bind off 3 sts at beginning of next 2 rows.

Bind off remaining 12 sts at once.

FINISHING

Pocket: With double strand of Victoria pick up and knit in twisted rib 17 sts for large pocket, work for 6 rows.

For small pocket, pick up and knit 13 sts work for 6 rows.

Work 3 rows of single crochet around entire work. Make a 2 st buttonhole 1″ from bottom and 3½″ apart.

Buttonhole: * Chain 2 sts, skip 2 * 5×.

Sew seams and insert sleeves.

Repeat single crochet and reverse crochet around sleeves.

Front

Back

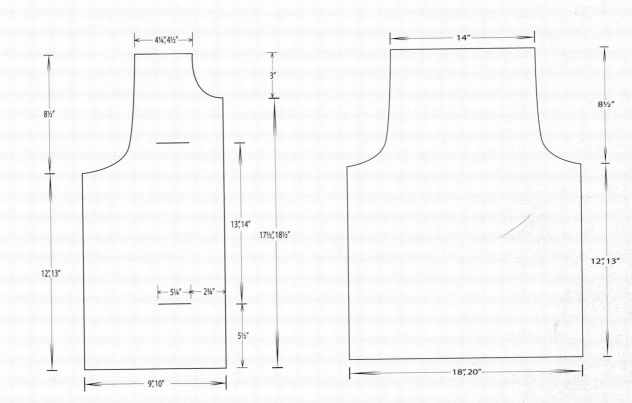

Sleeve

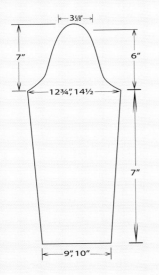

[*Tank*]

MATERIALS

4 (5) balls Anny Blatt
Angora Super

4 (5) balls Anny Blatt Victoria

NEEDLES

Size 6 and 7

Size 6 circular 16″

Crochet hook, size G

GAUGE

5.5 sts = 1″

7 rows–1″

STITCH

Stockinette

Twisted rib

ROW 1: K2, P2

ROW 2: P2, K2

ROW 3: Knit second st by
passing in back of first, then
remove both at the same time

ROW 4: P2, K2

FINISHED MEASUREMENT

Size 36 (38, 40)

With size 7 needles using Victoria cast on 94 (102, 106) sts.

Work in twisted rib for 2½″.

Change to Angora Super and stockinette and work until piece measures 12″ or desired length.

Change to size 6 needles and Victoria.

Work in twisted rib and start armhole shaping.

Bind off 5 sts at beginning of next 2 rows.

Bind off 2 sts at beginning of next 2 rows.

K2tog at each end of needle every other row 3x (7x, 9x).

When armhole measures 8½″ put all sts on stitch holder.

FRONT

Proceed as for back until armhole measures 5½″. Put center 18 sts on stitch holder.

Attach another ball of yarn, then at neck edge every other row bind off 3 sts 1x, 2 sts 1x, K2tog 4x.

When piece measures same as back put all sts on stitch holder.

FINISHING

With size 6 circular 16″ needles pick up and knit 102 sts. Continue in twisted rib matching and keeping continuity of established pattern.

Work for 3″.

Bind off in pattern.

Around armhole, single crochet 3 sts in a row, skip 1 st, continue all around followed by a row of reverse crochet.

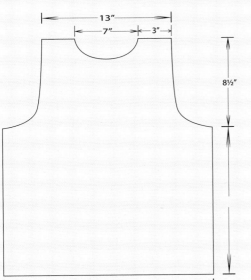

13″

7″   3″

8½″

18″ (19, 20)″

[*Summer Tank*]

MATERIAL

6 balls Mondial Tactel
2 stitch holders

NEEDLES

Size 4 and 7

GAUGE

6 sts = 1"

STITCH

Rib: K1, P1
Stockinette

FINISHED MEASUREMENT

Size 34/36

BACK AND FRONT

Cast on 210 sts with size 7 needle.

Work in K1, P1 rib for 7½".

K2tog, YO across the row.

Work in K1, P1 rib for 3 rows.

Bind off 90 sts.

FRONT

Continue on the next 120 sts. Decrease 30 sts evenly across the row to 90 sts.

Work 1 row in rib.

Left cup: Continue as follows in stockinette:

Decrease 6 sts on the first 40 sts. Increase 18 sts between sts 59 and 80 = 102 sts.

Work 3 rows in stockinette.

Place the first 34 sts on stitch holder.

Bind off 2 sts on right side every other row 5×, 1st 11×.

At the same time bind off on left side as follows: 7 sts 1×, then every other row K2tog 8×, then every row K2tog 26×.

When piece measures 5" place remaining 6 sts on stitch holder.

Right cup: Work to match left cup, reversing shaping by picking up 34 sts on holder and increasing to 68 sts.

Borders: With size 4 needles pick up 50 sts for inside borders of cups, K1, P1 for 5 rows.

Bind off in rib pattern.

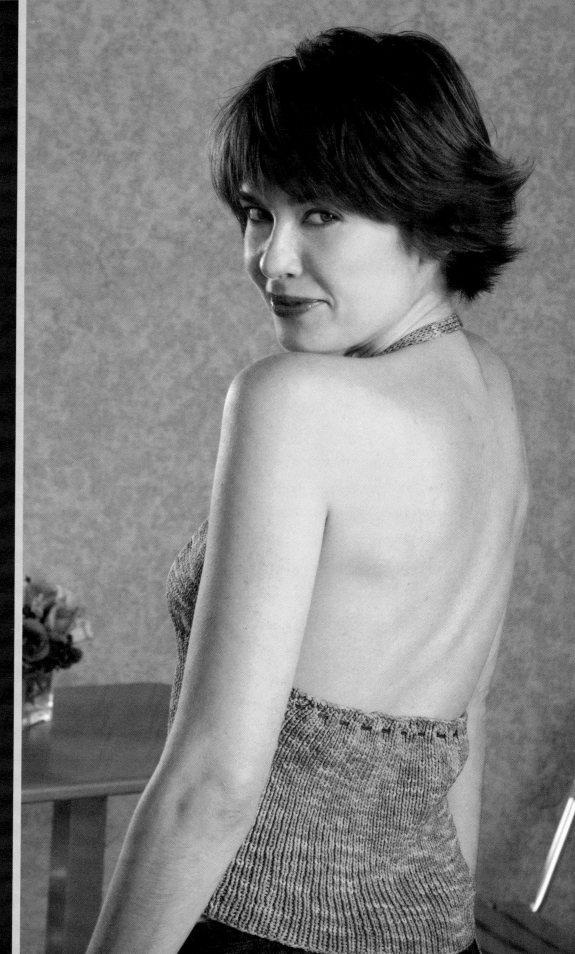

NECK BAND

Pick up and rib 6 sts left on holder and work for 10″.

Repeat on the 6 sts left on the second holder and join together with a three-needle bind-off.

Pull ribbon through eyelet.

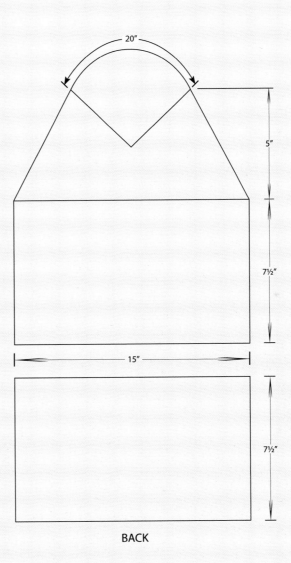

BACK

[*Edith's Pink Bikini*]

MATERIALS

3 balls Mondial Tactel
2 stitch holders

NEEDLES

Size 4 and 7

GAUGE

25 sts = 4″
37 rows = 4″

FINISHED MEASUREMENT

One size fits 6 to 10

BIKINI BOTTOM

Back: With size 7 needles cast on 9 sts. Work in stockinette until piece measures 1¼″. Increase 1 st at each end of needle every other row 32×. When piece measures 7″ place the remaining 73 sts on stitch holder.

Front: With size 7 needles cast on 9 sts. Work in stockinette until piece measures 1¼″. Increase 1 st at beginning and end of needle every 4 rows 4×, then every other row 21×. When piece measures 7″ place the remaining 59 sts on stitch holder.

FINISHING

Join crotch together. With size 4 needles pick up 140 sts around each leg and K1, P1 for 5 rows. Bind off.

BORDERS

Top: With size 4 needles cast on 7 sts. Pick up sts on holder, cast on 7 sts. K1, P1 for 1″. Bind off. Repeat same on other side.

BRA

I-Cord: With a double-pointed needle cast on 3 sts, knit 3 sts, push sts to front of needle, knit 3 sts. Do not turn work–repeat to desired length.

Left cup: Cast on 90 sts. Work 10 rows in rib, continue in stockinette. Decrease 6 sts on the first 40 sts. Increase 18 sts between sts 59 and 80 sts = 102 sts. Work 3 rows in stockinette, place 34 sts on holder.

Bind off on right side every other row 2 sts 5×, 1 st 11×. At the same time, at ½″ from border bind off on left side as follows: 7 sts 1× and work the last 4 sts on left YO, slip 1, K1, PSSO, P2, decreasing before these 4 sts every other row 8×, then every row 26×. Decrease by knitting 2 sts together or purling 2 sts together. When piece measures 5″ place remaining 6 sts on holder.

Right cup: Work to match left cup, reversing shaping by picking up 34 sts on holder and increasing to 68 sts.

Inside borders: With size 4 needles pick up 50 sts for inside borders of bra. K1, P1 for 5 rows. Bind off in rib.

Neck border: With size 4 needles pick up 6 sts on holder. Knit in garter for 9". Join to the remaining 6 sts on other cup and work three-needle bind-off. Join the 2 cups together. Decorate with either an appliqué flower or a button.

Cord: Either crochet I-cord or make a twist cord for 20". Make 4 pieces 9" long each for side closures.

[*Jacket*]

MATERIAL

20 balls (2 shades of brown, 10 skeins each) Katia Gatsby

2 yards Lang Piuma

5 buttons

5 stitch holders

NEEDLES

Size 10

Crochet hook, size H

GAUGE

4 sts = 1"

6 rows = 1"

STITCH

Seed stitch

FINISHED MEASUREMENT

Size 40

BACK

Cast on 80 sts with double yarn using 1 strand of each color.

Work in seed stitch until jacket measures 13".

ARMHOLE SHAPING

Bind off 4 sts at beginning of next 2 rows.

Bind off 2 sts at beginning of next 2 rows.

K2tog at each end of needle of every other row 6×.

When armhole measures 8½" put all sts on stitch holder.

FRONT

Make 2 pieces, reversing shapings.

Cast on 40 sts.

Work in seed stitch until piece measures same as back to armhole.

Start armhole shaping and neck decreases same as back, but on one side only.

At the same time start neck decreases as follows:

K2tog, then alternately (every 3rd row, every 4th row) 13× more for a total of 14 decreases.

When piece measures same as back put remaining 14 sts on stitch holder.

SLEEVES

Cast on 39 sts.

Work in seed stitch.

Increase 1 st at each end of needle every 12th row 6× = 51 sts.

When sleeve measures 17″ bind off 4 sts at beginning of next 2 rows.

Bind off 2 sts at beginning of next 2 rows.

K2tog at each end of needle every other row 7×.

When armhole measures 5¾″ bind off 2 sts at beginning of next 2 rows.

Bind off 3 sts at beginning of next 2 rows.

Bind off remaining 15 sts at once.

FINISHING

Single crochet all around front of sweater by * single crochet 3 sts in a row, skip 1*.

On second row of single crochet make 5 evenly spaced buttonholes. Make first buttonhole 1″ from bottom as follows: chain 2, skip 2. Finish with a crab stitch or reverse crochet.

Sew sweater, insert sleeves, and sew Piuma around bottom of sweater and sleeves.

Front

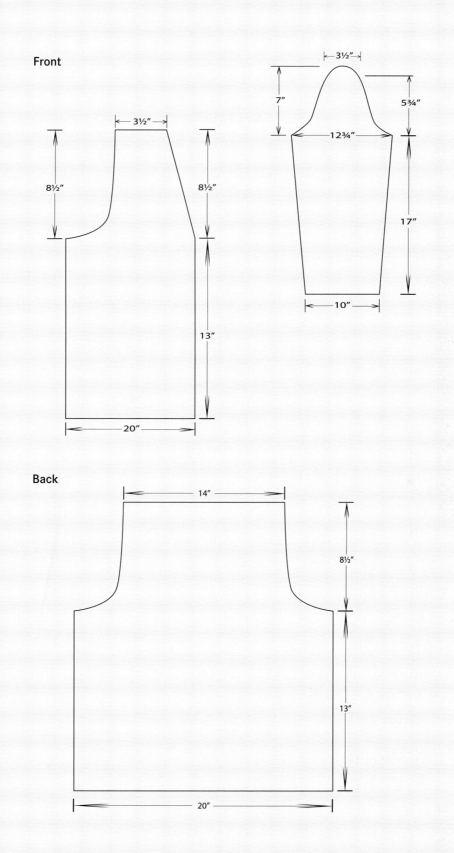

3½"

8½"

8½"

13"

20"

3½"

7"

5¾"

12¾"

17"

10"

Back

14"

8½"

13"

20"

[Dress]

MATERIAL

18 balls Katia Gatsby
(9 balls each of two different
browns. Yarn is doubled with
one strand of each color.)

5 stitch holders

NEEDLES

Size 9

Size 7 circular 16"

GAUGE

4½ sts = 1"

7 rows = 1"

STITCH

Stockinette

Seed stitch

FINISHED MEASUREMENT

Size 38, length 34½"

BACK

With size 9 needles cast on 77 sts.

Work in seed stitch for 4 rows.

Change to stockinette. Increase 1 st at each end of needle on every 33rd row 4× (85 sts).

When piece measures 21" start dart decreases as follows:

K21, slip 1, K1, PSSO, K1, K2tog, continue to the last 26 sts, slip 1, K1, PSSO, K1, K2tog, K21.

Knit 20 rows.

Repeat the dart decreases 1 more time.

When piece measures 26½" increase 1 st at end of every 8th row 4×.

When piece measures 34½" shape armholes.

Bind off 5 sts at beginning of next 2 rows.

Bind off 2 sts at beginning of next 2 rows.

K2tog at each end of needle every other row 5×.

When armhole measures 8½" put remaining 61 sts on stitch holder.

FRONT

Proceed same as back until armhole measures 5".

Put the center 23 sts on stitch holder.

Attach another ball of yarn. At neck edge every other row bind off 3 sts 1×, 2 sts 2×, K2tog every other row 2×.

When piece measures same as back put all sts on holder.

FINISHING

Join shoulder seams with a three-needle bind-off.

With size 7 circular 16″ needles pick up and knit 100 sts around neck. Work 6 rows in seed stitch.

Bind off loosely in seed stitch.

Pick up and knit 85 sts around each armhole.

Work 6 rows in seed stitch.

Bind off loosely in seed stitch.

Sew seams together.

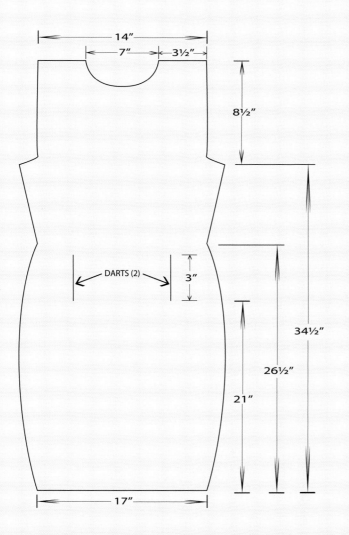

[*Pea Coat*]

MATERIAL

11 balls Noro Canna Cashmere

5 stitch holders

6 large buttons

1 small button

NEEDLE

Size 13

GAUGE

2.60 sts = 1″

4 rows = 1″

STITCH

Seed stitch

Stockinette

FINISHED MEASUREMENT

Sizes 41, 44

BACK

Cast on 55 (57) sts.

Work in seed stitch for 4 rows.

Continue in stockinette until piece measures 20½″.

ARMHOLE SHAPING

Bind off 3 sts at beginning of next 4 rows.

Bind off 2 sts at beginning of next 2 rows.

K2tog at beginning and end of needle 1× = 37 (39) sts.

When armhole measures 9½″ put all sts on stitch holder.

FRONT

Cast on 41 (43) sts.

Keeping the first 3 sts in seed, continue in stockinette on the remaining 38 (40) sts.

When piece measures 9½″ from beginning make a 3-stitch buttonhole every 6″.

BUTTONHOLE

Work 3 sts in seed. Leaving yarn on the right, slip 2 sts, pass 1st st over 2nd st (PSSO), slip 1 more st, PSSO, slip 1 more st, PSSO.

Turn work, move remaining st onto left-hand needle.

Cable cast on 3 sts.

Turn work and continue to last 17 sts. Split work for pocket opening.

Attach another ball of yarn, continue with two balls of yarn until split measures 6″. Then rejoin the two pieces and continue with one ball of yarn only.

When piece measures 20½″ bind off for armhole same as for back, but on one side only.

LAPELS

Change from stockinette to seed every other row 7× = 10 sts in seed. Then start increasing 1 st every other row 9× = 19 sts in seed.

When armhole measures 5½" bind off at the neck edge 17 sts 1×.

Bind off 3 sts 1×.

Every other row bind off 2 sts 2×.

Bind off 1 st 8×. When piece measures the same as back put remaining 12 sts on stitch holder.

Make another front, reversing shapings and making a buttonhole 17½" from start of work.

COLLAR

Pick up and knit 49 sts.

Work in seed stitch. Increase 1 st at each end of needle every other row.

Work until collar measures 3½".

Bind off loosely in seed stitch.

POCKETS

Pick up approximately 20 sts on the edge of pocket. Work in seed stitch for 1 inch.

SLEEVES

Cast on 31 (33) sts.

Work in seed stitch for 3 rows.

Change to stockinette.

Increase 1 st at each end on needle every 10th row 5× = 41 (43) sts.

When sleeve measures 17" or desired length bind off 3 sts at beginning of next 2 rows.

Bind off 2 sts at beginning of next 2 rows.

K2tog at each end of needle every other row 3× (4×).

When cap measures 6½″ bind off 2 sts at beginning of next 2 rows.

Bind off 3 sts at beginning of next 2 rows.

Bind off remaining 15 sts.

FINISHING

Sew side seams, insert sleeves, sew on buttons. Make two pocket linings.

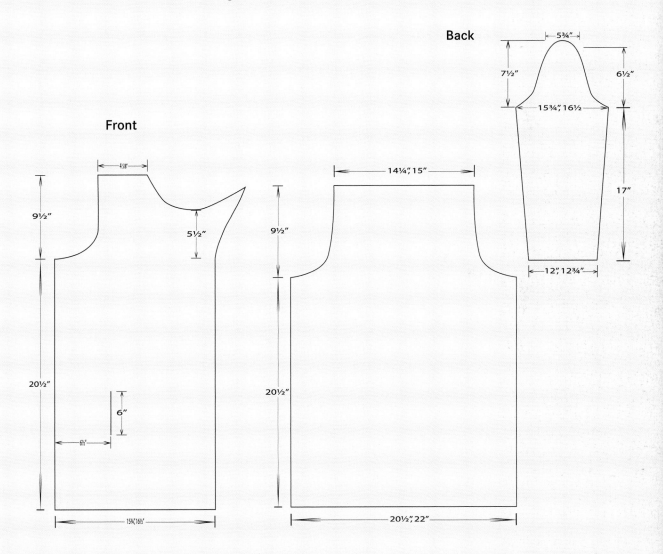

Front

Back

[Jacket in Lusso]

MATERIAL
14 skeins Fiesta Lusso
5 buttons
4 stitch holders

NEEDLES
Size 10½
Crochet hook, size H

GAUGE
3.5 sts = 1″
4 rows = 1″

FINISHED MEASUREMENT
Size 39

Pattern is a multiple of 2 sts + 1.

ROW 1: Right side. K1 through back loop (tbl) across the row to end.

ROW 2: K1 * P1 tbl, K1 * to end.

ROW 3: P1 * K1 tbl, P1 * to end.

ROW 4: Same as row 2.

ROW 5: Same as row 1.

ROW 6: P1 tbl * K1, P1 tbl * to end.

ROW 7: * K1 tbl, P1 * to end.

ROW 8: Same as row 6.

Repeat rows 1 through 8 for pattern.

BACK

Cast on 69 sts.

Proceed in pattern until piece measures 12″ or desired length.

ARMHOLE SHAPING

Bind off 4 sts at beginning of next 2 rows.

Bind off 2 sts at beginning of next 2 rows.

K2tog at each end of needle every other row 4×.

When armhole measures 8½″ put all sts on stitch holder.

FRONTS

Make 2 pieces, reversing all shapings.

Cast on 35 sts. Work in pattern to armhole.

Shape armhole on one side only. At the same time shape neck.

K2tog at neck edge, then alternately (every 2nd row, every 3rd row) 12× more.

When armhole measures same as back put all sts on holder.

SLEEVE

Cast on 35 sts. Increase 1 st at each end of needle every 10th row 5× (45 sts).

When sleeve measures 17" or desired length bind off 4 sts at beginning of next 2 rows.

Bind off 2 sts at beginning of next 2 rows.

K2tog every other row 5×.

When cap measures 6" bind off 2 sts at beginning of next 2 rows.

Bind off 3 sts at beginning of next 2 rows.

Bind off remaining 13 sts at once.

FINISHING

Join shoulder seams with a three-needle bind-off.

Sew seams. Insert sleeves.

Single crochet for 2 rows, making buttonholes evenly spaced on the 3rd row. The 1st one is approximately ½" from bottom.

Single crochet for 2 rows followed with 1 row of reverse crochet around the whole sweater.

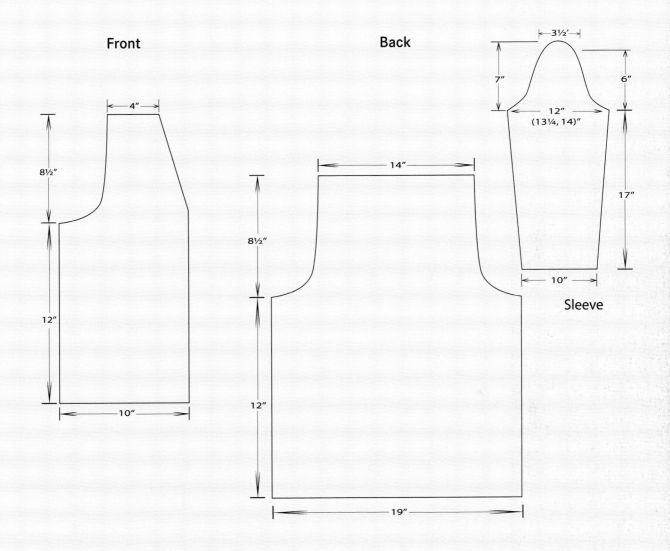

Front

Back

4"

8½"

12"

10"

14"

8½"

12"

19"

Sleeve

3½"

7"

6"

12"
(13¼, 14)"

17"

10"

[*Skirt in Lusso*]

MATERIAL

9 skeins Fiesta Lusso
Elastic for waistband

NEEDLES

Size 10½
Size 9 circular 24"

GAUGE

3.5 sts = 1"
4 rows = 1"

FINISHED MEASUREMENT

Size 8/10

FRONT

Pattern is a multiple of 2 sts + 1.

Cast on 60 sts. Work in pattern as follows:

ROW 1: Right side. K1 through back loop (tbl) across the row to end.

ROW 2: K1 * P1 tbl, K1 * to end.

ROW 3: P1 * K1 tbl, P1 * to end.

ROW 4: Same as row 2.

ROW 5: Same as row 1.

ROW 6: P1 tbl * K1, P1 tbl * to end.

ROW 7: * K1 tbl, P1 * to end.

ROW 8: Same as row 6.

Repeat rows 1 through 8 for pattern.

Increase 1 st at each end of needle every 4" 3× (66 sts). Continue until piece measures 24". Put all sts on stitch holder.

BACK

Repeat same as front.

FINISHING

Sew both seams. With size 9 circular needles pick up sts left on holders. Join, careful not to twist the sts. Purl 1 row across all sts. K1, P1 for 1". Purl 1 row. P1, K1 for 1". Fold band and sew, leaving a 1" opening. Thread elastic through.

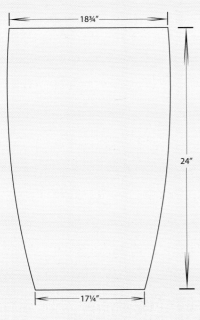

18¾"

24"

17¼"

[*Tank in Tenero*]

MATERIAL

4 skeins Fiesta Tenero

4 stitch holders

NEEDLES

Size 11

Crochet hook, size H

GAUGE

2.4 sts = 1"

4½ rows = 1"

STITCH

Stockinette

FINISHED MEASUREMENT

Size 39

BACK

Cast on 46 sts, work in stockinette for 11½".

ARMHOLE SHAPING

Bind off 3 sts at beginning of next 2 rows. Bind off 2 sts at beginning of next 2 rows. Knit 2 sts together at beginning and end of needle every other row 2x. When armhole measures 8½" put all sts on stitch holder.

FRONT

Proceed same as back until armhole measures 5½". Bind off the center 8 sts. Attach another ball of yarn, then every other row bind off 2 sts 2x, 1 st 1x.

FINISHING

Join shoulder seams with a three-needle bind-off. Sew seams. Single crochet around neck and armhole followed with a reverse crochet or crab stitch.

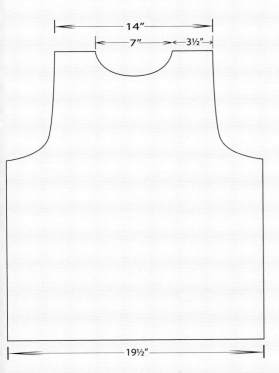

14"

7" 3½"

19½"

[*Afghan in Stuff*]

MATERIAL

2½ skeins Prism Stuff, three different colors

1 skein in two colors Classic Elite Playful Weekend

1 skein Judi & Co. Kringle

NEEDLE

Size 13 circular 32″

GAUGE

2.80 sts = 1″

FINISHED MEASUREMENT

48″ × 60″

With Playful Weekend color 1 cast on 135 sts. Work 4 rows in garter.

Change to first skein of Stuff.

Work in pattern as follows:

Pattern is a multiple of 6 + 3 sts.

ROW 1: (RS) P3 * K3, YO, P3 * repeat from * to * to end.

ROW 2: K3 * P4, K3 * repeat to end.

ROW 3: P3 * K1, K2tog, YO, K1, P3 * repeat to end.

ROW 4: K3 * P2, P2tog, K3 * repeat to end.

ROW 5: P3 * K1, YO, K2tog, P3 * repeat to end.

ROW 6: K3 * P3, K3 * repeat to end.

Repeat rows 1 through 6 until the skein of Stuff is totally used up.

Change to Kringle and work P1 * YO, P2tog *, P1 for 4 rows.

Knit 2 rows in garter, increase 2 sts on last row.

Change to second color of Stuff and work ½ skein.

Multiple of 6 + 5 sts.

ROW 1: K4 * YO, slip 1, K2tog, PSSO, YO, K3 * repeat, finish with K1.

ROW 2: Purl.

ROW 3: K1 * YO, slip 1, K2tog, PSSO, YO, K3 * YO, slip 1, K2tog, PSSO, YO, K1.

ROW 4: Purl.

Change to Playful Weekend color 2.

Work 4 rows P1 * YO, P2tog * repeat to end. End with P1.

Knit 2 rows in garter, increase 4 sts on last row.

Change to third color of Stuff.

Afghan in Stuff

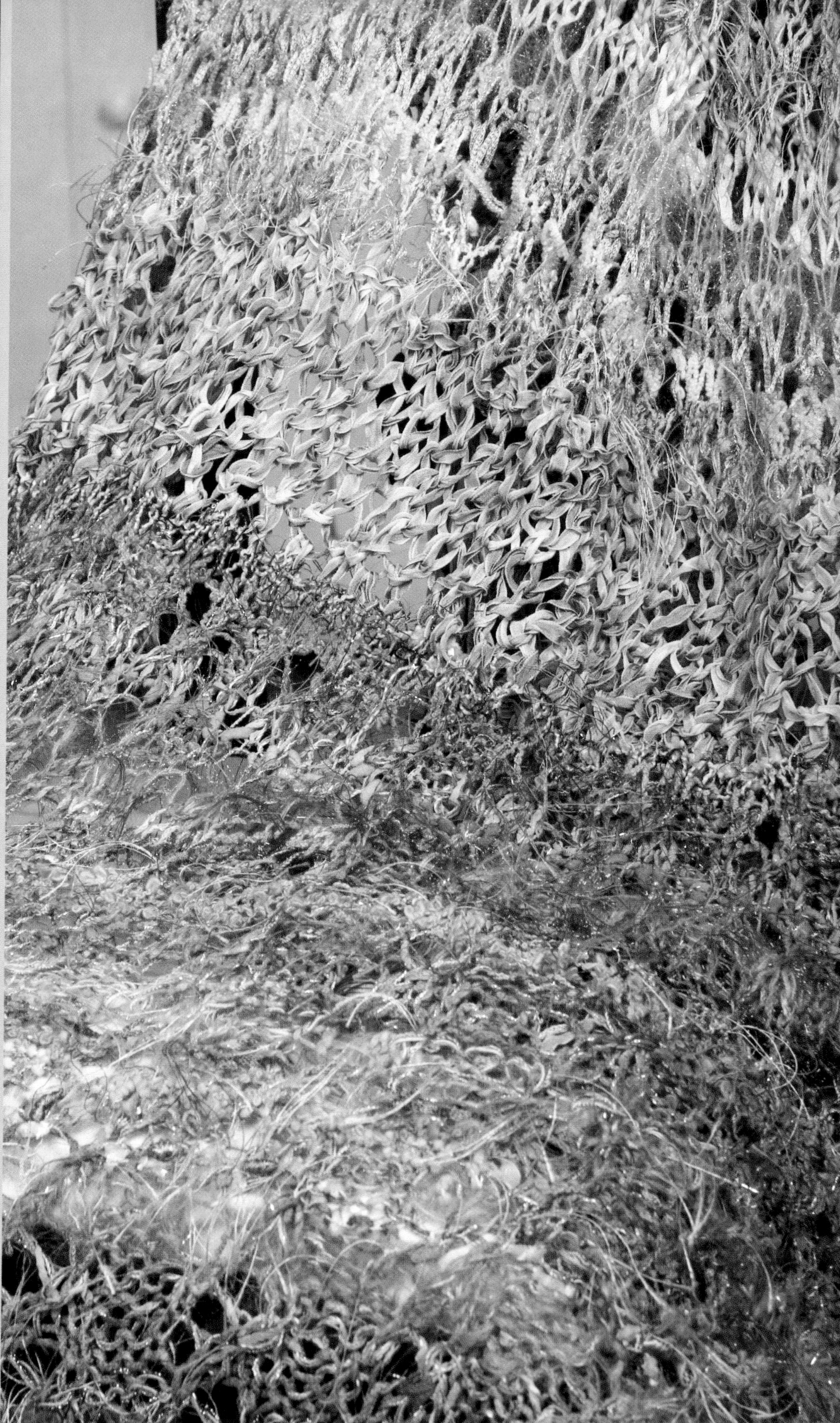

Multiple of 8 + 5 sts.

ROW 1: K3 * YO, K2, P3tog, k2, YO, K1 * K2.

ROW 2: Purl.

ROW 3: Same as row 1.

ROW 4: Same as row 2.

ROW 5: Same as row 1.

ROW 6: Same as row 2.

ROW 7: K2, P2tog * K2, YO, K1, YO, K2, P3tog * to the last 9 sts, K2, YO, K1, YO, K2, P2tog, P2.

ROW 8: Purl.

ROW 9: Same as row 7.

ROW 10: Purl.

ROW 11: Same as row 7.

ROW 12: Purl.

Repeat rows 1 through 12 until the end of skein.

Change to Playful Weekend, decrease 6 sts evenly across the row.

Knit 4 rows. Bind off loosely.

Using all leftover yarn, cut fringes in 20″ pieces (4 pieces for each fringe).

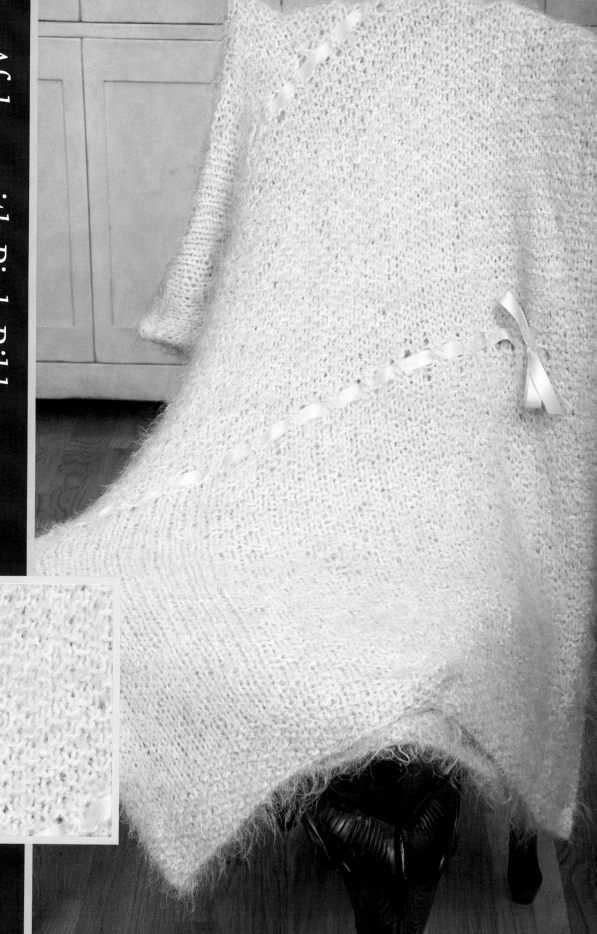

[*Afghan with Pink Ribbon*]

MATERIALS

20 balls GGH Amelie

1 package stitch markers

7 yards ribbon

NEEDLE

Size 13 circular 32″

GAUGE

3 sts = 1″

STITCH

Garter

Stockinette

Seed stitch

Checkerboard:

ROW 1: K2, P2

ROW 2: K2, P2

ROW 3: P2, K2

ROW 4: P2, K2

Eyelet: K2tog, YO (bring yarn in front as if to purl but knit)

FINISHED MEASUREMENT

48½″ × 60″

Cast on 146 sts.

Work in seed stitch for 2½ inches.

Knit 7 sts in seed, place marker, knit 44 sts in checkerboard pattern, place marker, knit 44 sts in garter, place marker, knit 44 sts in stockinette, place marker, knit 7 sts in seed.

Proceed in this manner until piece measures 14″.

Knit 4 rows in garter, 1 row in eyelet, 4 rows in garter.

Next row: 7 sts in seed, 44 sts in stockinette, 44 sts in checkerboard, 44 sts in garter, 7 sts in seed.

When piece measures 14″ knit 4 rows in garter, 1 row in eyelet, 4 rows in garter.

Next row: 7 sts in seed, 44 sts in garter, 44 sts in stockinette, 44 sts in checkerboard, 7 sts in seed. Work for another 14″.

Work 4 rows in garter, 1 row in eyelet, 4 rows in garter.

Next row: 7 sts in seed, 44 sts in checkerboard, 44 sts in garter, 44 sts in stockinette, 7 sts in seed.

Work for 14″.

Work in seed stitch for 2½″.

Bind off loosely.

Weave ribbons into eyelets.

[*Multicolor Poncho*]

MATERIAL

1 ball each:
Pingouin Talisman, pink
Diva, white
Gedifra Tecno Hair, pink,
yellow, green
Prism Bubble pink
Prism Super Dazzle, pastel
Trendsetter Aura, pink
Anny Blatt Bijou, pink
Lang Charm, green
Lynx, yellow
Schachenmayr La Nova, purple
Katia Gatsby pink, purple
Alba, pink, green
Cubetto, green
Lana Grossa Pep, pink

NEEDLES

Size 11
Crochet hook, size H

GAUGE

3.50 sts = 1″

STITCH

Stockinette
Garter

FINISHED MEASUREMENT

20″ × 28″

Stockinette: knit 1 row, purl 1 row.

Garter: knit all rows.

Double wrap: wrapping yarn around both needles, knit a stitch.

Seed stitch:

ROW 1: Knit 1, purl 1.

ROW 2: Knit the purl, purl the knit.

Checkerboard:

ROW 1: * K3, P3 * across the row.

ROW 2: * K3, P3 * across the row.

ROW 3: * P3, K3 * across the row.

ROW 4: * P3, K3 * across the row.

Single crochet, reverse crochet.

Make 2 pieces. Sides do not have to match.

SIDE 1

Cast on 70 sts with La Nova purple, work 2 rows in stockinette.

Change to Cubetto green, work 8 rows in garter.

Change to Tecno Hair yellow, work 6 rows in garter.

Change to Lynx double strands, work 4 rows in garter, 6 rows in stockinette, 1 row double wrap, 6 rows in stockinette, 4 rows in garter.

Change to Super Dazzle and work as follows: K1 * YO, K2tog * K1 across the row. Work 3 rows in garter.

Change to Pep, work 8 rows in garter.

Change to Bubble, work 8 rows in garter.

Change to Diva (white) and Gatsby pink together, work 6 rows in stockinette, 1 row double wrap, 6 rows in stockinette.

Change to Tecno Hair green, work 8 rows in garter.

Change to Alba green, work 4 rows in garter, 1 row double wrap, 4 rows in garter.

Change to Aura, K1 * YO K2tog * K1 across the row.

Change to Gatsby pink and purple, 1 strand each, work 4 rows in seed stitch.

Bind off loosely in seed stitch.

SIDE 2

Cast on 70 sts with pink Alba, work 6 rows in seed stitch.

Change to Diva, work 4 rows in garter, 1 row double wrap, 4 rows in garter.

Change to Tecno Hair green, work 6 rows in garter.

Change to Bijou, work 3 rows in stockinette, 4 rows in garter, 1 row double wrap, 4 rows in garter, 3 rows in stockinette.

Change to La Nova, work 7 rows in stockinette, 4 rows in garter, 1 row double wrap, 4 rows in garter, 7 rows in stockinette.

Change to Super Dazzle, work 8 rows in seed stitch.

Change to Cubetto, work 8 rows in garter.

Change to Bubble, work 6 rows in garter.

Change to Lynx double strands, work 6 rows in garter.

Change to Tecno Hair green, work 6 rows in garter.

Change to Charm, work 4 rows in garter, 3 rows in stockinette, 1 row double wrap, 3 rows in stockinette, 4 rows in garter.

Change to Talisman, work 4 rows in stockinette, 4 rows in checkerboard of 3 sts, 4 rows in stockinette.

Change to Gatsby pink and purple, 1 strand each, work 8 rows in seed stitch.

Bind off loosely in seed stitch.

FINISHING

With pink Alba single crochet around followed with 1 row of reverse crochet or crab stitch.

Cut fringes using all colors and place them closely together.

Sew pieces following diagram.

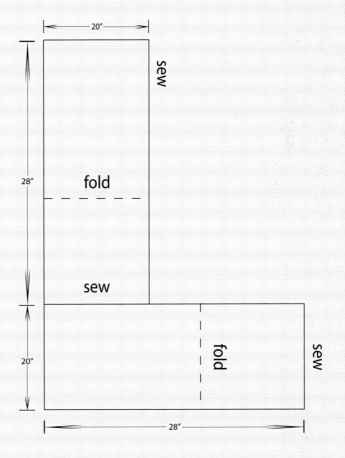

[*Rust Poncho*]

MATERIAL

1 ball each:
GGH Cascade, black, brown, khaki, green, light rust, rust
Gedifra Distrato, green
Muench String of Pearls, multi (orange, pink, green), multi (purple to green)
Gedifra, Costa Rica
Bouton d'Or Opale, purple, khaki, multi purple
Prism Super Dazzle, two colors
Prism, Bonbon
Berroco, Glitz

NEEDLES

Size 11
Crochet hook, size H

GAUGE

3.20 sts = 1″

STITCH

Garter
Dropped garter
Stockinette

FINISHED MEASUREMENT

Made in two pieces, each 20″ × 28″

SIDE 1

With Cascade black cast on 64 sts. Knit 4 rows in garter.

Change to Cascade brown, knit 4 rows.

Change to String of Pearls, work 8 rows in stockinette.

Change to Distrato, work 12 rows in stockinette.

Change to Costa Rica, knit 4 rows in garter.

Change to Cascade rust, knit 4 rows in garter.

Change to Opale purple, work 4 rows in stockinette.

ROW 1: Add Cascade rust and proceed as follows: * knit 2 sts in Opale purple, knit 2 sts in rust *. Repeat across the row.

ROW 2: Purl across in same manner.

ROW 3: * Knit 2 sts in rust, 2 sts in purple *.

ROW 4: Purl across in same manner.

Change to Opale purple, work 4 rows in stockinette.

Change to Opale multi, work 5 rows in stockinette.

Change to Cascade light rust, work 6 rows in stockinette.

Change to Super Dazzle, work 6 rows in stockinette.

Change to Opale khaki, work 4 rows in garter.

Work 4 rows in stockinette.

Work 1 row wrapping yarn twice around each stitch.

Work 1 row in garter.

Work 4 rows in stockinette.

Work 4 rows in garter.

Change to Costa Rica, work 4 rows in garter.

Change to String of Pearls, work 14 rows in stockinette.

Change to Bonbon, work 6 rows in stockinette.

Change to Glitz, work 6 rows in stockinette.

Change to Opale purple, work 4 rows in garter, 6 rows in stockinette, 4 rows in garter.

Change to Opale multi, work 4 rows in garter.

Bind off loosely.

SIDE 2

With Cascade black cast on 64 sts, knit 4 rows in garter.

Work 4 rows in stockinette.

Change to Cascade brown, work 4 rows in stockinette.

Change to Super Dazzle, work 6 rows in stockinette.

Change to String of Pearls purple to green multi, work 10 rows in stockinette.

Change to Opale purple, work 4 rows in garter.

Work 6 rows in stockinette.

Work 1 row in dropped stitch.

Work 4 rows in garter.

Change to Opale multi, work 4 rows in garter.

Change to Costa Rica, work 6 rows in garter.

Change to Cascade khaki, work 10 rows in stockinette.

Change to Cascade green, work 12 rows in stockinette.

Change to Distrato, work 12 rows in stockinette.

Change to Costa Rica, work 2 rows in garter.

Change to Cascade rust, work 4 rows in garter, 6 rows in stockinette, 4 rows in garter.

Change to Super Dazzle, work 7 rows in stockinette.

Change to Bonbon, work 5 rows in stockinette.

Change to Glitz, work 6 rows in stockinette.

Bind off loosely.

FINISHING

Join pieces (see diagram). Single crochet one row around the neck with Cascade black, followed by one row of crab stitch.

Make 10″ fringes using one strand of each of the leftover yarns.

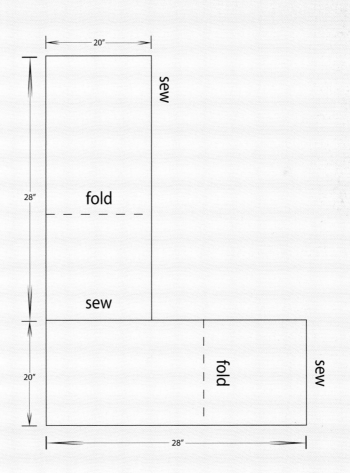

[*Shrug*]

MATERIAL

2 balls Prism Dover

½ skein Prism Stuff

1 ball Muench String of Pearls

NEEDLES

Size 10½ and 11

Crochet hook, size G

GAUGE

4 sts = 1"

5¾ rows = 1"

STITCH

Stockinette

Garter

FINISHED MEASUREMENT

13" × 56"

With size 10½ needles and String of Pearls cast on 100 sts.

Knit 2 rows in garter.

Change to Stuff.

Decrease to 32 sts, then every other row increase 1 st at each end of needle 9× = 50 sts. Work until piece measures 8".

Change to Dover and work until piece measures 18" from beginning.

Change to size 11 needles, work for 20".

Change to size 10½ needles, work for 10".

Change to Stuff and work for 8", then start decreasing every other row to 32 sts.

Change to String of Pearls and increase to 100 sts.

Knit 2 rows in garter.

Bind off loosely.

FINISHING

With String of Pearls single crochet all around body opening followed with a row of reverse crochet. Sew 18" on both sides for sleeves.

[*Tank*]

MATERIALS

3 balls Prism Dover
1 ball Muench String of Pearls
5 stitch holders

NEEDLE

Size 10½

GAUGE

4 sts = 1″
5¾ rows = 1″

STITCH

Garter
Stockinette

FINISHED MEASUREMENT

Size 34 (38, 42)

BACK

With String of Pearls cast on 136 (152, 168) sts.

Work 1 row in garter.

Next row: K2tog across the row = 68 (76, 84) sts.

Join Dover and continue in stockinette for 11″ (12″, 13″) or desired length.

ARMHOLE SHAPING

Bind off 4 sts at beginning of next 2 rows.

Bind off 2 sts at beginning of next 2 rows.

K2tog at each end of needle every other row 2× (6×, 7×). When armhole measures 8½″ put all sts on stitch holder.

FRONT

Work same as back until armhole measures 4″.

Put center 20 sts on holder.

Attach another ball of yarn.

At neck edge and every other row bind off 3 sts 1×, 2 sts 1×, K2tog
1×. When piece measures same as back put remaining 10 sts on holder for each shoulder.

FINISHING

Join shoulder seams with a three-needle bind-off.

With String of Pearls pick up and knit 95 sts around neck.

Next row: increase 1 st in every st as you purl the row.

Bind off loosely.

Armhole: with String of Pearls pick up and knit * 3 sts in a row, skip 1.
* Repeat from * to * across the row.

Next row: purl, increasing 1 every st.

Bind off loosely.

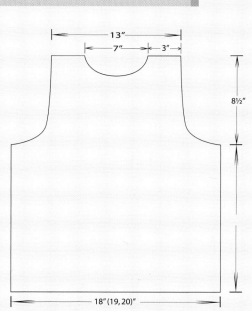

[*Jacket*]

MATERIAL

1 ball Trendsetter Segue

7 balls (8 balls) Trendsetter Essence

3 buttons

5 stitch holders

NEEDLES

Size 11

Crochet hook, size I

GAUGE

2.35 sts = 1"

2.30 rows = 1"

STITCH

Stockinette

Reverse stockinette

FINISHED MEASUREMENT

Size 36 (40)

BACK

Cast on 42 (46) sts. Work in stockinette until piece measures 13" or desired length.

ARMHOLE SHAPING

Bind off 2 sts at beginning of next 4 rows.

K2tog at beginning and end of needle every other row 1× (2×).

When armhole measures 8½" put all sts on stitch holder.

FRONT

Make 2 pieces, reversing all shapings.

Cast on 21 (23) sts.

Work in stockinette to armhole shaping.

Bind off 2 sts at beginning of next row, purl 1 row.

Bind off 2 sts at beginning of next row.

K2tog at armhole edge 1× (2×).

For reverse shaping, all shapings are made at beginning of purl row. At the same time, at neck edge K2tog or P2tog alternately every 3rd (4th) row 6× (7×).

When piece measures same size as back put all sts on stitch holder.

SLEEVES

Cast on 20 (22) sts, work in stockinette. Increase 1 st at each end of needle every 7th row 4× (5×).

When sleeve measures 17" or desired length bind off 2 sts at beginning of next 4 rows.

K2tog at each end of every other row 1× (3×).

When cap measures 5½" bind off 2 sts at beginning of next 2 rows.

Bind off 3 sts at beginning of next 2 rows.

Bind off remaining 8 sts at once.

FINISHING

With Segue single crochet in front edge for 6 rows.

Make a buttonhole on right side on 3rd row, the first one 1" from bottom, then 2 more every 5".

Buttonhole: Chain 3 sts, skip 3 sts.

Sew seams. Reverse stockinette will be the right side for sleeves only.

HINT

Buttonhole on right side as women are always right.

Finish with a single crochet all around, including bottom of jacket.

Follow with a reverse crochet or crab stitch.

Repeat single crochet or crab stitch around sleeve edges.

Front

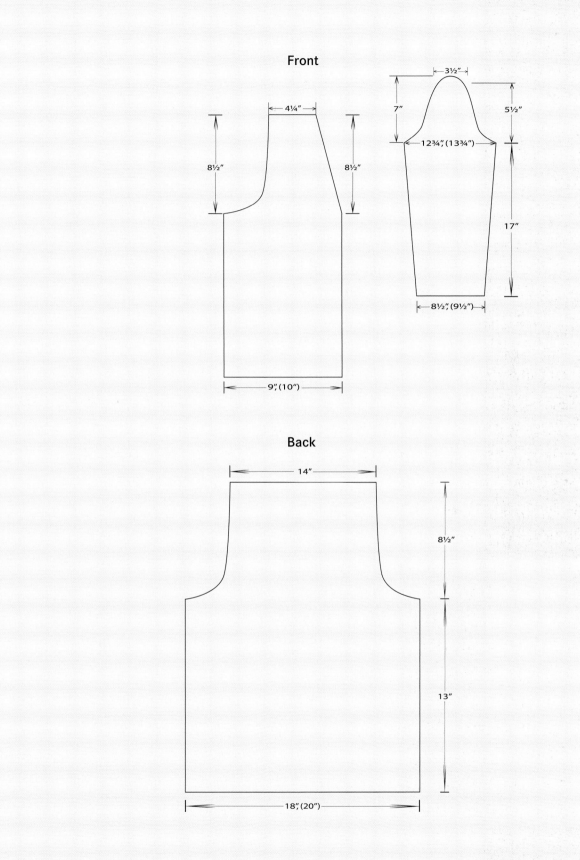

4¼"

8½"   8½"

9" (10")

3½"

7"   5½"

12¾" (13¾")

17"

8½" (9½")

Back

14"

8½"

13"

18" (20")

[*Skirt*]

MATERIAL

1 ball Trendsetter Segue
4 balls Trendsetter Essence
Elastic ¾" wide

NEEDLE

Size 10½ circular 24"

GAUGE

2.60 sts = 1"
3 rows = 1"

STITCH

Stockinette
Seed stitch

FINISHED MEASUREMENTS

Bottom 32" round
Top 38"
Length 24"

Cast on 84 sts, knit 42 sts, place marker, knit 42 sts, place marker. Join, careful not to twist sts.

Increase 1 st before and after each marker every 5" 4×.

When skirt measures 23¼" from beginning change to Trendsetter Segue and seed stitch for ¾", change to stockinette for ¾".

Bind off loosely.

Fold waistband, sew elastic.

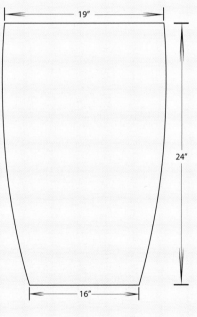

[*Tank*]

MATERIAL
5 (6) balls Trendsetter Segue
5 stitch holders

NEEDLES
Size 13
Size 11 circular 16″

GAUGE
3 sts = 1″
5 rows = 1″

STITCH
Seed stitch

FINISHED MEASUREMENT
Size 36 (38, 42)

BACK

Cast on 53 (57, 63) sts. Work in seed stitch until piece measures 11″ (11½″, 13″).

ARMHOLE SHAPING

Bind off 3 sts at beginning of next 2 rows.

Bind off 2 sts at beginning of next 2 rows. K2tog at each end of every other row 2x (4x, 4x).

When armhole measures 8½″ put all remaining 39 (39, 42) sts on stitch holder.

FRONT

Proceed same as back until armhole measures 3″ less than back.

Put the center 11 sts on stitch holder.

Attach another ball of yarn. At neck edge every other row bind off 3 sts 1x, 2 sts 1x.

K2tog every other row 1x. When piece measures same as back put all sts on holder.

FINISHING

Join shoulder seams together with a three-needle bind-off.

With size 11 needles pick up and knit 57 sts around neck. Work in seed stitch for 1½″.

Bind off loosely in pattern.

Single crochet 1 row around each armhole and around bottom of sweater.

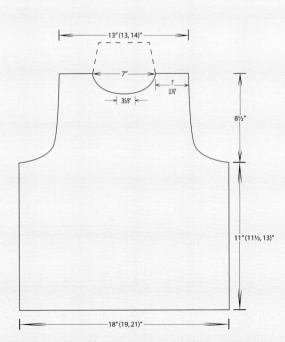

13″ (13, 14)″
7″
7″ (1¾″)
35/8″
8½″
11″ (11½, 13)″
18″ (19, 21)″

Natalie Eig

[*Angora Super Poncho*]

MATERIAL

4 balls Anny Blatt
Angora Super

5 skeins Anny Blatt Victoria

1 package stitch markers

NEEDLES

Crochet hooks, sizes I and N

STITCH

Single crochet (sc)

Double crochet (dc)

With 1 strand of Victoria and 1 strand of Angora Super and smaller hook, chain 38".

Join with a slip stitch, careful not to twist. Place marker.

Sc in each stitch all around.

Start pattern:

ROUND 1: Dc in 1st st, chain 1, dc in the same st. Place marker in that st. * Chain 1, dc, skip 1 st. *

Repeat from * to * to the middle of round. Dc, chain 1, dc all in the same st. Mark that st. Repeat until the end of round.

ROUND 2: Dc, chain 1, dc in the first arch, * chain 1, dc, skip 1 st *, repeat to second marked st. Dc, chain 1, dc in the same arch. Repeat from * to * until end of round.

Repeat round 2 one more time. Change to larger hook. Keep repeating round 2 to desired length.

With smaller hook, tighten up neckline to desired width by sc as follows: * 3 sc in a row, skip 1 chain *.

FINISHING

With Victoria only, cut fringes to desired length. In our model we used 10" fringes.

[*Poncho with Feather Trim*]

MATERIAL

14 balls Adrienne Vittadini
Fiora, used double throughout

2 yards Lang Piuma

1 package stitch markers

NEEDLES

Crochet hooks, sizes I and N

STITCH

Single crochet (sc)

Double crochet (dc)

With 2 strands of Fiora and smaller hook, chain 40". Join with a slip stitch, careful not to twist. Place marker.

Sc in each stitch all around.

Start Pattern:

ROUND 1: Dc in 1st st, chain 1, dc in the same st. Place marker in that st. * Chain 1, dc, skip 1 st. *

Repeat from * to * to the middle of round. Dc, chain 1, dc all in the same st. Mark that st. Repeat until the end of round.

ROUND 2: Dc, chain 1, dc in the first arch, * chain 1, dc, skip 1 st *, repeat to second marked st. Dc, chain 1, dc in the same arch. Repeat from * to * until the end of round.

Repeat round 2 one more time. Change to larger hook. Keep repeating round 2 to desired length.

With smaller hook, tighten up neckline to desired width by sc as follows: * 3 sc in a row, skip 1 chain *.

FINISHING

Sew Piuma along bottom edge of poncho.

Poncho with Crystal Beads

MATERIAL

3 balls Anny Blatt Muguet,
2 light, 1 dark of the
same color family

600 crystal beads

1 package stitch markers

NEEDLE

Crochet hook, size I

With 2 strands of Muguet, same color, chain 38". Join, careful not to twist. Place marker.

Single crochet in each chain.

ROUND 1: * Chain 7, skip 7 * across round.

ROUND 2: * Chain 7, skip 3, join in 4th chain, skip 3, chain 7 * repeat from * to * across round.

ROUND 3: Repeat round 2.

ROUND 4: Chain 9, repeat as above.

Work 3 rows, same as round 4.

ROUND 8: Chain 11.

Work 3 rows even.

ROUND 12: Chain 13, work 2 rounds.

ROUND 14: Change to 2 strands of darker color, work 2 rounds. Fasten off.

With 2 strands of darker color, tighten up neck, if necessary, with a single crochet, 3 sts in a row, skip 1.

String beads, about 22 in each arch, forming arches at bottom of work.

Abbreviations: The "language" of knitting. Directions are abbreviated into an easy-to-follow code, such as K2P2.

Backstitch: One of the three methods of seaming a sweater we cover in the book.

Binding Off: The final stage of knitting, where you "close" off the live stitches and take your knitting off the needle.

Binding Off in Pattern: When knitting in rib or another pattern stitch, you must bind off in pattern (i.e., if you see a knit stitch, you knit; if a purl, you purl; and bind off accordingly).

Blocking: The method of adding structure to your knitting by drying it in shape after either steaming it or submerging it in a warm water bath.

Bobbins: Used in fair isle or intarsia knitting to control several different colored strands of yarn.

Buttonhole: I teach the one-row method which produces a neater, firmer button hole than other methods.

Cable: A repetitive vertical pattern created by crossing two or more stitches back and forth across two or more other stitches.

Cabling Needle: When working a cable, the stitches that are being crossed are slipped onto this needle and held either in front of or behind the other stitches until it is time to knit them.

Cast On: The process of creating your first row of stitches. There are several methods; I teach the two-balls cast-on.

Circular Needles: Double-pointed needles that are fixed to each end of a long flexible piece of nylon or metal cord. They can be used to create a seamless, tubular piece of knitting.

Continental Style: I teach "English" style; this is the "other" style of knitting. It's tricky, though it can be fast once mastered.

Crochet Hook: Crochet uses one needle with a hooked end to create a fabric. It can be useful to finish your knitting or to add borders.

Decrease: The process of reducing the number of stitches on your needles. I teach a few methods, and care must be taken to select the correct one, as the decreases slant the stitches and can affect the look of your knitting.

Double-Pointed Needles: Used to create a tubular fabric, such as socks. They can work a much smaller number of stitches than circular needles, which make them useful for finishing projects begun on circular needles, such as hats.

Drop Stitch: A dropped stitch that has been worked deliberately for a visual effect, leaving a long "ladder" above it.

Dropped Stitch: A stitch that has been accidentally dropped, creating a run in your knitting. You must pick up the stitch before you continue knitting.

Ease: Sweaters are designed with varying amounts of ease, or room. A sweater designed to fit a 36-inch bust might actually measure 38 inches because of ease.

Felting: A very popular technique, whereby knitting is agitated in hot water and the fibers form a thick, "felted" fabric. Used primarily for bags, mittens, and slippers.

Full Fashioning: A very sophisticated way to work the decreases on a sweater, which adds a noticeable outline to the armhole and shoulder shaping.

Garter: Knit on both sides.

Gauge: The number of stitches per inch and per row. This is the crucial secret to successful knitting—you must achieve the correct gauge for your pattern.

Increases: Adding stitches in order to shape a garment.

Knit: One of two fundamental stitches, the other being the purl.

Knitwise: Insert the needle into the stitch as though you are going to knit it.

Lace: An openwork design, based around a repetitive pattern, that resembles lace. YOs and K2tog are used together to achieve this effect.

Make One: My preferred method for increasing the number of stitches on your needle.

Mattress Stitch: This is the main method of seaming I use, and I also refer to it as "weaving," because that is essentially what you do.

Needles: The core of your knitting kit, these are available in many materials and styles, such as bamboo, metal, plastic, circular, and double-pointed.

Patterns: Patterns can be written out in words or presented in a more visual charted form. Either way, once you know how to read them, you'll be able to knit them.

Picking Up Stitches: A technique most often used on necklines, where you use your needle to draw a strand of yarn through the bound-off stitches at the top of your pattern pieces. These stitches are then knitted "up" to form a neckband.

Purl: The second fundamental stitch.

Purlwise: Insert the needle into the stitch as though you are going to purl it.

Repeats: In order to correctly read a knitting pattern you must understand that not every stitch will be written out—if the same stitch is worked over and over again it will be written K2*K2P2*. The portion between the asterisks is repeated till the end of the row, unless specified otherwise.

Seaming: The method by which you join the separate pieces of your knitting together. I teach three methods: mattress, backstitch, and three-needle bind-off.

Seed Stitch: Knit and purl stitches are alternated in the same row, then in the second row you knit over the purl stitches and purl over the knit stitches.

Shaping: Using decreases and increases to add curves and shape to your knitting, especially around the hips, waist, and bust.

Slip Stitch: This is where you slip a stitch from the left needle to the right needle rather than knit or purl it. It is often used for a decorative effect.

Stitch Holder: Essentially a very large safety pin, this is used to hold live stitches that are not being worked.

Stockinette: Knit one row, purl one row.

Substitutions: Patterns usually specify a yarn, but you can always substitute a different yarn—just make sure you can obtain the correct gauge with it.

Swatches: A four-by-four-inch sample of knitting completed prior to beginning a project, it is used to ensure that your gauge is correct and that your yarn and pattern work well together.

Yarn Over: The process of wrapping your yarn around the needle to add another stitch with a lacy effect.

abbreviations

K: Knit

P: Purl

tog: together

YO: Yarn Over

DP: Double-Pointed Needle

SL: Slip

dec: decrease

inc: increase

st: stitch

SKP: Slip, Knit, Pass

PSSO: Pass Slipped Stitch Over

K2tog: Knit Two Together

P2tog: Purl Two Together

CN: Cable Needle

FOLL: Following

M1: Make One

MC: Main Color

PM: Place Marker

LKS: Local Knitting Shop

RS: Right Side

WS: Wrong Side

tbl: through back loop

sc: single crochet

dc: double crochet

Repeat Directions Following
As many times as indicated.

( ): Repeat directions inside of parentheses as many times as indicated.

knitting needle table

US	METRIC (UK)	US	METRIC (UK)
0	2mm	9	5.5mm
1	2.25mm	10	6mm
2	2.75mm	10½	6.5mm
3	3.25mm	11	8mm
4	3.5mm	13	9mm
5	3.75mm	15	10mm
6	4mm	17	12.75mm
7	4.5mm	19	15mm
8	5mm	35	19mm

resource list

La Knitterie Parisienne
12642 Ventura Blvd.
Studio City, CA 91604
(818) 766-1515
(800) 228-9927

Anny Blatt USA Inc.
7796 Boardwalk
Brighton, MI 48116
(800) 531-9276

Berroco Inc.
14 Elmdale Rd.
Uxbridge, MA 01569
(800) 343-4948

Bouton D'Or
7796 Boardwalk
Brighton, MI 48116
(800) 531-9276

Brookman Imports/Plassard
  Yarns
4911 Lyons Tech Parkway,
Suite 30
Coconut Creek, FL 33073
(866) 341-9425

Bryson Distributing
745 Fillmore
Eugene, OR 97407
(800) 544-8992

Classic Elite Yarns Inc.
122 Western Ave.
Lowell, MA 01851
(800) 444-5648

Clover Needlecraft Inc.
13438 Alondra Blvd.
Cerritos, CA 90703
(800) 233-1703

Euro Yarns Inc.
P.O. Box 336
Amityville, NY 11701
(800) 645-3457

Fiesta Yarns
5401 San Diego NE, Suite A
Albuquerque, NM 87113
(877) 834-3782

JCA Inc.
35 Scales Lane
Townsend, MA 01469
(800) 225-6340

Karabella Yarns Inc.
1201 Broadway
New York, NY 10001
(800) 550-0898

Knitting Fever Inc.
P.O. Box 336
Amityville, NY 11701
(800) 645-3457

Lang
14 Elmdale Rd.
Uxbridge, MA 01569
(800) 343-4948

Muench Yarns
1323 Scott St.
Petaluma, CA 94954
(800) 733-9276

Prism Arts Inc.
3140 39th Ave. North
St. Petersburg, FL 33714
(877) 805-1487

Rowan Yarns
4 Townsend West #8
Nashua, NH 03063
(800) 445-9276

Skacel Collection Inc.
P.O. Box 88110
Seattle, WA 98138
(800) 255-1278

Tahki-Stacy Charles Inc.
70-30 80th St. Bldg. 36
Ridgewood, NY 11385
(800) 338-9276

Trendsetter Yarns
16745 Saticoy St. #101
Van Nuys, CA 91406
(800) 446-2425

Unicorn Books & Crafts Inc.
1338 Ross Street
Petaluma, CA 94954
(800) 289-9276

Unique Kolours Ltd.
28 N. Bacton Hill Rd.
Malvern, PA 19355
(800) 252-3934

index

Page numbers in *italics* refer to photographs and illustrations.

A

acrylics, 43
Adrienne Vittadini Fiora, 207
afghans:
   9/11 celebrity, 76
   patterns, 178–81, *178, 180,*
     182–83, 182
Alba, 185
alpaca, 43
alterations:
   for bust/chest measurement,
     50–51
   for neckline, 50–52, *52*
   for sleeve length, 49–50, *50*
   for sweater length, 56, *56–57*
   using short rows, 87–88
angora, 41–42
Anny Blatt:
   Angora Super, 107, 125, 145,
     149, 205
   Bijou, 185
   Muquet, 209
   Victoria, 125, 145, 149, 205
arms, armholes, 48, 50, *50*
   see also sleeves
Arquette, Patricia, 39
Artful Cinema, 127
arthritis, 5
auxiliary needle, *see* cable
   needle

B

baby-blanket party, 72–74
baby blankets, 114–15, *114,*
   116–17, 116
back, 48
back cable, 32
backstitching, 61, 62
bags, 118–21, *118, 120, 121,*
   122–23, 122
Bateman, Justine, vii, 38, 76
beginners:
   patterns for, 8
   yarns for, 4–5
Berroco, 46, 189
Big Kureyon, 101
bikinis, 154–57, *154, 156*
binding off, 14, *15*
   in decreasing, 30
   three-needle, 62–63, *63*
blankets, 72–74, 76, 82, 114–17,
   114, 116
blocking, 60
   see also shaping
blocking boards, 64
blocking pins, 64
bobbins, *6*
bobbles, 88
Bonbon, 189
borders, 52, 58
Bouton D'Or:
   Angora, 127
   Dune, 106
   Opale, 189
bust/chest, 48, 50–51, 87–88
buttonholes, 52–54, *54–55, 58*

C

cable cast on, 34, *34*

cable needles, *6,* 32

cabling, 32–35, *33*

Canvas Pad, The, x, *x,* 70

capelet, 110–11, *110, 111*

cardigans, 51, 58

Carr, Jan, 46

cashmere, 42

casting on, 8–9, *9*

cast-on edge, 12

checkerboard stitch, 183

chenille, 43

circular needles, *6*

Classic Elite:

    Forbidden, 100

    Playful Weekend, 179

cleaning, 65, 66

Clover Needles, 5, 46, 72

coats, 46

    pea, 166–69, *166, 169*

Colinette Giotto, 95

Coppola, Sophia, vi, 13, 18, 76

cotton, 39–40

crew necks, 51, 52, *52*

crochet hooks, *7,* 16

crochet shell stitch, 115

Cubetto, 185

D

Davis, Kristin, 23

Debbie Bliss Baby Cashmerino, 44

decreasing, 28, 30, *31,* 34

    full fashion, 30

    see also alterations

diaper bags, 118–21, *118, 120, 121*

Diva, 185

DK Cotton, 109

double crochet stitch, 205, 207

double wrap stitch, 113

dresses, 134–35, *134, 135,* 162–65, *162, 165*

dropped quarter stitch, 99, 189

dropped stitches, 16–19, *17*

dye lots, 38, 44

E

Eig, Audrey, 72, *98, 107, 128, 144, 148, 192, 207, 208*

Eig, Merrill, xi, 81

Eig, Natalie, 72, *102, 103, 106, 112, 170, 174, 176, 204*

embroidery floss, 62

Eucalan, 65, 66

eyelash yarn, 43, 82

eyelet stitch, 183

F

Fanning, Dakota, vi, 75

felted bags, 82

felting, 5, 67, 82

Fiesta:

    Lusso, 171, 175

Tenero, 177
finishing, 60–68
finishing pins, *6*
flash cards, 34
flex needles, *6*
4–stitch cable, 32
front cable, 32
furs, 43

G

garter stitch, 12, 18, 20, 94, 95,
  99, 104, 113, 115, 119, 183,
  185, 189, 193, 195
gauges, 3, 5, 21, 23–25,
  39, 49
  see also sample swatches
Gedifra:
  Calista, 103, 105
  Costa Rica, 189
  Distrato, 189
  Tecno Hair, 109, 117, 185
Gellar, Sarah Michelle, 45
GGH:
  Amelie, 183
  Cascade, 189
gift knitting kits, 83
Glitz, 189
glossary of terms, 210–13
Goa yarns, 73
Gorham, Anel Lopez, *96, 124, 136,*
  184
Gorham, Christopher, 76, *101*

H

Hana Silk, 46
hand bag, 122–23, *122*
Hannah, Daryl, vi, 19, 76
hats, 104–5, *104,* 106, *106,* 107,
  107
Hennesy, Carolyn, *110, 130, 138,*
  140
hip, 48

I

increasing, 28, *29,* 34
  see also alterations

J

jackets, 144–47, *144,* 147, 158–
  61, *158, 160, 161,* 170–73,
  170, 173, 196–99, *196, 197,*
  199
Judi & Co. Kringle, 179

K

Karabella Magic, 127
Katia:
  Gatsby, 159, 163, 185
  Ingenua, 111
  Ola, 115
  Scala, 95
kids, 44, 74
Kleinman, Shellie, *100, 126*

knit stitch, 10–11, *11,* 23, 34
  purl stitch vs., 12, *12*
knitting:
  for babies, 44, 73, 118–21,
    114–17
  basics of, 1–20
  for boys, 74
  for charity, 75–76
  creativity in, 85–90
  emotional benefits of, 68,
    69–76, 86
  gift ideas for, 81–84
  health benefits of, 86, 87
  for kids, 44, 74
  for pets, 82
  social benefits of, 69–76, 77
    80
  technique of, 47–58
  for teens, 44
knitting bags, 7
knitting experts, 3
knitting needle gauge, 6, *7*
knitting needle table, 215
knitting notebook, 39
knitting social, 71–72
knit tips, 2, 3, 4, 5, 10, 12, 14, 16,
    18, 19, 20, 24, 25, 28, 30, 32,
    34, 38, 39, 40, 41, 42, 44, 45,
    48, 50, 58, 60, 62, 64, 65, 66,
    68, 83
Krakowski, Jane, 73

L

La Knitterie Parisienne, xi-xiv, *xii,*
    2–5, 8, 22, 46, 69–70, 77–80,
    80, 82, 91–93
Lana Grossa Pep, 185
Lang:
  Charm, 185
  Furore, 117
  Piuma, 137, 159, 207
  Roma, 139, 141
lanolin, 65
Lapchinski, Semara, *116*
learn to knit kit, 3–7
lengthening, 56, *56–57*
Leo (dog), *114*
Lockhart, Jane, 40
Loeb, Lisa, 88
looping *see* worming
Lynx, 185

M

make one, 28
Mandel Bread, 80
Manheim, Camryn, 72–74, 76
mattress stitch, *see* weaving
measurements:
  in adapting patterns, 49
  altering for bust, 50
  armhole, 50
  of personal figure, 48
  retro, 51
  see also alteration

mercerized cotton, 40

merino wool, 5, 40

Merison, Tal, 68

Messing, Debra, 71, 76, 82

microfibers, 43

Miller, J. Robin, *97, 150, 152*

mistake rib stitch, 101

mistakes, correction of, 58,
    66–68

mohair, 41

Mondial:
    Kross, 103, 105
    Paglia di Firenze, 123
    Tactel, 151, 155

Moore, Julianne, vi, 84, 76

Muench String of Pearls, 189,
    193, 195

Mullally, Megan, 11

N

neck, neckline, 48, 50–52, *52,*
    58

needle cases, 5

needle holders, *7*

needle size, *see* gauge

needles, 3, 5, *5, 7,* 10
    bamboo, 4, 5, 72
    cable, *6*
    circular, *6,* 68
    Clover, 5, 46, 72
    darning, 62
    flex, *6*
    plastic, 4

for sewing, 6, *7,* 62

table of, 215

U.S. vs. metric, 5, 25

9/11 celebrity afghans, 76

Noro, 46
    Canna cashmere, 113, 167
    Cashmel, 137
    Iro, 101
    Kureyon, 94

novelty yarns, 43–44, 82

O

Okada, Mr., 46

Olsen, Mary Kate and Ashley,
    86

OnLine Clip, 131

Oprah, 75

O'Toole, Annette, vi-vii, 76, 78

P

paint chip palette, 83

Parker, Sarah Jessica, 23

patterns, 47–58, 91–209
    adaptation of, 49–50
    afghan, 178–81, *178, 180,*
        182–83, *182*
    bikini, 154–57, *154, 156*
    blanket, 114–17, *114, 116*
    capelet, 110–11, *110, 111*
    diaper bag, 118–21, *118, 119,*
        120, 121

dress, 134–35, *134, 135,* 162–65, *162, 165*

hand bag, 122–23, *122*

hat, 104–5, *104,* 106, *106,* 107, *107*

jacket, 144–47, *144,* 147, 158–61, *158, 160, 161,* 170–73, *170,* 173, 196–99, *196, 197, 199*

pea coat, 166–69, *166, 169*

poncho, 112–13, *112, 113,* 138–39, *138, 139,* 184–91, *184, 187, 188, 191,* 204–9, *204, 206, 207, 208*

reading of, 48

scarf, 94, *94,* 95, *95,* 96, *96,* 97, *97,* 98–99, *98,* 100, *100,* 101, *101,* 102–3, *102*

shawl, 126–27, *126*

shrug, 108–9, *108, 109,* 124–25, *124,* 192–95, *192, 184, 195*

skirt, 174–75, *174, 175*

suit, 170–77, *170, 173, 174, 175, 176, 177,* 196–203, *196, 198, 199, 200, 201, 202, 203*

sweater, 130–33, *130, 132, 133*

tank top, 128–29, *128, 129,* 136–37, *136, 137,* 140–43, *140, 143,* 148–49, *148, 149,* 150–53, *150, 152, 153,* 176–77, *176, 177,* 194–95, *194, 195,* 203–4, *203, 204*

pea coat, 166–69, *166, 169*

pearl cotton thread, 62

Pecan Triangles, 79

Pingouin Talisman, 185

point protectors, 6, *6*

ponchos, 82, 112–13, *112, 113,* 138–39, *138, 139,* 184–91, *184, 187, 188, 191,* 204–9, *204, 206, 207, 208*

Prism:
 Bubble, 185
 Dover, 193, 195
 Stuff, 179, 193
 Super Dazzle, 185, 189

projects, *see* patterns

Pronto yarns, 73

puckering, 14

pulling in, 8

pulling out, 8

pure wool, 41

purl stitches, 12–13, *13,* 23, 34
 distinguishing knit stitches from, 12, *12*

R

rabbit fur, 100

Rebeck, Theresa, 19

recipes, 79–80

reknitting, 58

resource list, 216–17

reverse stitch, 111

reverse stockinette stitch, 197

Rhea, Caroline, vi, 71, 72–73, 76

ribbing, 23, 25, 26, *27*
 changing colors in, 28

rib stitch, 107, 125

right side, 12, 13

ripping, 3, 8, 18, 20, 26, 41

round necks, 52, *52*

Rowan Kid Classic, 97

Rowan yarns, 44

Rule of 3, 52

running, 16

S

sample swatches, *7*

  see also gauges

scarves, 8, 23, 82, 94, *94,* 95, *95,*
    96, *96,* 97, *97,* 98–99, *98,* 100,
    100, 101, *101,* 102–3, *102*

Schachenmayr:

  La Nova, 185

  Pompon, 103, 105

schematics, 48, 64

Schnoll, Nancy, *108, 188*

scissors, 3, 6, *7*

seaming, 60–63, *61,* 65

seed stitch, 100, 107, 113, 117,
    167, 183, 201, 203

  see backstitching; finishing;
    weaving

shaping, 23, 28–31, 60, 87–88

shawls, 82, 126–27, *126*

shedding, 42

Shields, Brooke, 72, 74

shortening:

  of sleeves, 49

  of sweaters, 56, *56–57*

short rows, 87–88

shrinking, 5, 40

  in angora, 42

  see also felting

shrugs, 108–9, *108, 109,* 124–25,
    124, 192–95, *184, 192, 195*

single crochet stitch, 115, 205,
    207, 209

sip and knit, 77–80, *80*

Sirdar Funky Fur, 115

Sirdar Snowflake Chunky, 115

6–stitch cable, 32

Skacel Fiori, 99

skirts, 174–75, *174, 175, 200,
    201*

sleeves, 49–50, *50*

  see also arms, armholes

slipknots, 14

Spolar Levine, Antoinette, 76, *94,
    95, 126, 166*

Stacy Charles Twist, 127

steaming, 65

stitch counters (gauge), *7,* 10

stitch counters (row), 6–7, *7*

stitches:

  checkerboard, 183

  crochet shell, 115

  double crochet, 205, 207

  double wrap, 113

  dropped garter, 99, 189

  eyelet, 183

  garter, 12, 18, 20, 94, 95, 99,
    104, 113, 115, 119, 183, 185,
    189, 193, 195

knit, 10–11, *11,* 23, 34

mistake rib, 101

purl, 12–13, *13,* 23, 34

reverse, 111

reverse stockinette, 197

rib, 107, 125

seed, 100, 107, 113, 117, 167,
183, 201, 203

single crochet, 115, 205, 207, 209

stockinette, 12, 109, 111, 113,
117, 119, 125, 167, 177, 183,
185, 189, 193, 195, 197, 201

twisted rib, 100

stitch holders, 6, *6,* 64, *64*

stitch markers, 6, *6*

stretching, 40

suits, 170–77, *170, 173, 174, 175,
176, 177,* 196–203, *196, 198,
199, 200, 201, 202, 203*

superwash, 39

sweaters:

blocking of, 64–65

cleaning of, 65–66

copying and recreating, 89–90

finishing of, 59–68

knitting of, 48–58

length of, 48, 56

patterns for, 130–33, *130, 132, 133*

vintage, 89

T

Tahki Chat, 119

tank tops, 128–29, *128, 129,*

136–37, *136, 137,* 140–43, *140,
143,* 148–49, *148, 149,*
150–53, *150, 152, 153,* 176–77,
176, 177, 194–95, *194, 195,*
203–4, *203, 204*

tape measures, 3, 6, *6, 7,* 23

tension control, 8, 12, 23

texture, 88

three-needle bind off, 62–63,
63

Tolsky, Susan, 71

tools, 3–7

Trendsetter:

Aura, 106, 185

Bloom, 96

Emmy, 129

Essence, 197, 201

Eyelash, 94, 95

Segue, 116, 135, 197, 201,
203

Willow, 109

Zucca, 106

12–stitch cable, 32

twisted rib stitch, 100

U

upknitting, 19

V

virgin wool, 41

V-necks, 58

W

waist, 48

Wall, Mary, *122, 134, 158, 162, 196, 200*

washing, *see* cleaning

weaving, 60–61, *61*

Williams, Regina, 46

Wilson, Carnie, 3, *3,* 71, *118, 206*

wool, 4–5, 40–41

  merino, 5, 40

  tapestry, 62

worming, 43

wrist, 48

wrong side, 12, 13

Y

yarn bras, *6*

yarn labels, 25, 39

yarn needles, 6, *7*

yarn shops, 3

yarns, 4, 37–46

  adding balls of, 14

  for adults, 45

  for babies, 43, 44

  for beginners, 4–5

  characteristics of, 39

  cost of, 4

  hand-dyed, 45

  inexpensive, 40–41

  for knitting vs. sewing, 62

  leftover, 38

  manmade, 39

  novelty, 43–44

  ribbon, 45

  for teens, 44

  textured, 45

  unravelling of, 44

  weight of, 4

  see also specific types of yarn